ANALYZING THE ISSUES

CRITICAL PERSPECTIVES ON
DIGITAL
MONOPOLIES

Edited by Jennifer Peters

Enslow Publishing

101 W. 23rd Street
Suite 240
New York, NY 10011
USA

enslow.com

Published in 2019 by Enslow Publishing, LLC
101 W. 23rd Street, Suite 240, New York, NY 10011

Library of Congress Cataloging-in-Publication Data

Names: Peters, Jennifer author.
Title: Critical perspectives on digital monopolies / Jennifer Peters.
Description: New York : Enslow Publishing, [2019] | Series: Analyzing the
issues | Audience: Grades 7-12. | Includes bibliographical references and
index.
Identifiers: LCCN 2018000688| ISBN 9780766098480 (library bound) | ISBN
9780766098497 (pbk.)
Subjects: LCSH: Google (Firm)—Juvenile literature. | Amazon.com (Firm)
—Juvenile literature. | Internet industry—Juvenile literature. |
Monopolies—Juvenile literature.
Classification: LCC HF5548.323.G66 P48 2019 | DDC 338.7/61025040973—
dc23
LC record available at https://lccn.loc.gov/2018000688

Printed in the United States of America

To Our Readers: We have done our best to make sure all website addresses
in this book were active and appropriate when we went to press. However,
the author and the publisher have no control over and assume no
liability for the material available on those websites or on any websites
they may link to. Any comments or suggestions can be sent by email to
customerservice@enslow.com.

Excerpts and articles have been reproduced with the permission of the
copyright holders.

Photo Credits: Cover, Sdecoret/Shutterstock.com; cover and interior
pages graphics Thaiview/Shutterstock.com (cover top, pp. 1, 4-5), gbreezy/
Shutterstock.com (magnifying glass), Ghornstern/Shutterstock.com
(interior pages).

CONTENTS

INTRODUCTION

America has long had a strong position against monopolies. Also known as trusts, monopolies are situations in which one or a few businesses control an industry. It all started with the Interstate Commerce Act of 1887, which was designed to open up the railroad industry. This position was further enhanced by the Sherman Antitrust Act of 1890, which allowed the government to intervene if it believed a company had earned a monopoly through force rather than through merit and the will of the consumer.

While these laws sound old and outdated, antitrust laws are more relevant today than ever before, and that's because of digital monopolies. What is a digital monopoly? Well, there are a lot of different businesses that have been accused of participating in monopolistic behavior in the digital world. Apple has faced monopoly charges because of Apple Music and allegations that it encouraged record labels not to partner with other digital streaming services. Amazon has been accused of creating a monopoly over e-books, or electronic books, because of the fact that it made it harder for people to buy e-books by only selling files that are compatible with its Kindle products. Google and Facebook have been accused of having a duopoly over online advertising because they take approximately 80 percent of the advertising money spent on digital ads campaigns. And those are just a few of the issues that have arisen in the twenty-first century.

Now, you might be wondering why it even matters if a company has a monopoly over a particular industry. But monopolies often hurt consumers. Think about it this way: if you get $100 for your birthday, and you want to buy some new video games or DVDs, you want to get more for your money. Lucky for you, you can go to multiple stores, both in person and online, and find the best price for what you want to buy. Maybe one store has a sale on video games, so you can get two for the price of one, or you can buy them from an online store that's offering you free shipping. Because all these options exist, you get to choose how to spend your money. But if only one store sold video games, you'd have to pay whatever price they set, even if it was unfair. If a company has a monopoly, they can charge whatever they want and set any terms for consumers that they choose, and they don't have to do what's best for their customers.

Online, these monopolies mean that you might not get to use the internet the way you want to because one company has decided that they would like things to work a certain way. It means you can only stream music from one company, or you can only share your photos on one website. And as more and more of our lives take place online, it's important to know what your options are and how to make sure the digital world operates as freely as the physical world. The articles presented in this book examine how various people, governments, and groups are addressing the pitfalls of digital monopolies today.

CHAPTER 1

WHAT THE EXPERTS SAY

Experts and academics don't always agree on what constitutes a monopoly. Some believe that all monopolies are the product of the market, and therefore they're not really a problem. Others believe that any monopoly, even one created by consumer choice, is a bad thing and hurts the economy and the consumers. Most, however, agree that digital monopolies are particularly dangerous, especially given the lack of legal regulation of the internet. As you read what different experts have to say, you can consider the consequences of digital monopolies—as well as the possible benefits.

EXCERPT FROM "PRINCIPLES OF MICROECONOMICS," BY EMMA HUTCHINSON, FROM THE UNIVERSITY OF VICTORIA, 2016

8.1 MONOPOLY

Whereas perfect competition is a market where firms have no market power and they simply respond to the market price, a monopolistic market is one with no competition at all, and firms have complete market power. In the case of **monopoly**, one firm produces all of the output in a market. Since a monopoly faces no significant competition, it can charge any price it wishes. While a monopoly, by definition, refers to a single firm, in practice, the term is often used to describe a market in which one firm has a very high market share.

Even though there are very few true monopolies in existence, we deal with some every day, often without realizing it: your electric and garbage collection companies for example. Some new drugs are produced by only one pharmaceutical firm—and no close substitutes for that drug may exist.

While a monopoly must be concerned about whether consumers will purchase its products or spend their money on something altogether different, the monopolist need not worry about the actions of other firms. As a result, a monopoly is not a price taker like a perfectly competitive firm. Rather, it exercises power to choose its market price.

SINGLE PRICE MONOPOLY

So we know a competitive market faces an elastic demand, what about a **single-priced monopoly**? This is distinct from other monopolies in that the firm must charge the same price to all consumers. In this case, the aggregate demand is the firm's demand! To explore monopoly, consider the sunglasses market.

What do Oakley, Ray-Ban and Persol have in common? They are all owned by the same brand. That's right, Luxottica, an Italian based eyewear company, produces about 70% of all name brand eyewear. This is fairly close to a monopoly, as with that high of a market share, Luxottica dominates the market price. Notice that Luxottica is not a single price monopoly, as it practices a form of price discrimination by having multiple brands aimed at different consumers. Let's consider what would happen if Luxottica only sold one kind of sunglasses at the same price to all consumers, and if they owned 100% of the market.

Whereas the competitive firm was a small player in the aggregate market, the monopolist dictates both the final price and the quantity. If Luxottica decides to lower price, it must do so for ALL buyers. Consider what implications this has on revenue.

...

According to the law of demand, as price falls, quantity demanded increases. This means that Luxottica can increase revenue by lowering price, as they sell more sunglasses. This is not that happens from a price decrease however, as the firm decreases price it loses some of the revenue on the goods it was previously selling. ... For a monopoly, a price decrease doesn't always result in more revenue. When price is decreased, we have a loss in revenue from existing sales, and an increase in revenue from new sales. The more sales we are making, the greater the loss. ...

REPRESENTING REVENUE

As we can see, finding where price = MC [marginal cost] would no longer be a good metric for where we should produce, since we also want to take into account the affect price changes have on revenue. While the above analysis seems rather random, we can systematically represent the changes in revenue from a decrease in price — in fact, we already have! In Topic 4, we explored how the elasticity at different points along a demand curve affected the changes in revenue.

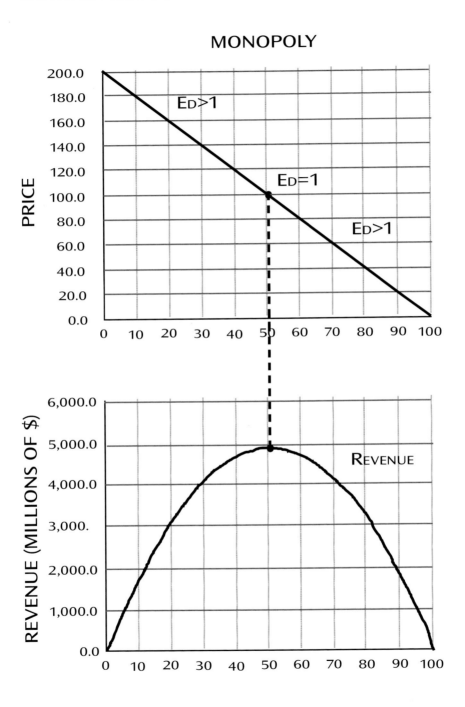

FIGURE 8.1D

Remember, the equation to calculate elasticity is (% change in quantity/% change in price). Looking at the two changes in revenue from the examples above, we can see that the *decrease* in revenue came from the *price change*, and the *increase* came from the *quantity change*. This means that when % change in quantity > % change in price, our revenue increases from a price drop! ...

So, does this mean Luxottica will produce 50 million pairs of sunglasses, charge $100 per unit and call it a day? Not necessarily. While that would maximize revenue, remember that it doesn't matter if revenue is rising if costs are rising by more. To find where we produce, we must find the point where marginal revenue = marginal cost. ...

MONOPOLY BEHAVIOR

So what price will Luxottica charge? Adding its marginal cost to the graph, we can see that MC= MR at 30 million sunglasses. At any quantity below this, MR > MC meaning Luxottica can increase profits by increasing production.

MR and MC intersect where P = $80, will this be the market price? At 30 million sunglasses sold, consumers are willing to pay $140 per pair. Luxottica knows this and will charge as high as it can. This means the market price will be $140.

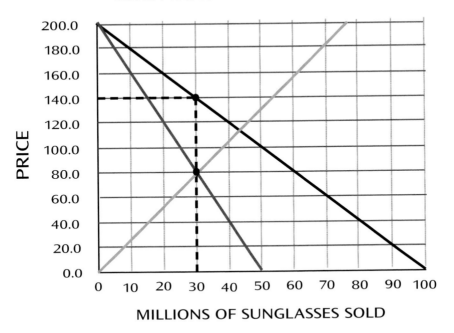

LUXOTTICA'S PRODUCTION DECISION

MILLIONS OF SUNGLASSES SOLD

FIGURE 8.1F

This behaviour is standard for a monopolist. Operate at the quantity where MC = MR, and charge a price equal to the consumers willingness to pay.

MARKET SURPLUS

In earlier topics, a key metric we analyzed was market/ social surplus, which showed how government inter- vention can cause deadweight loss or correct the loss from externalities, etc. In this case, we want to see if a monopoly is as efficient as perfect competition. Recall our rule that differences in *prices* from equilibrium cause *transfers* and differences in *quantity* from equilibrium cause *deadweight loss*. Make a prediction as to how the monopoly market will affect efficiency. ...

DEADWEIGHT LOSS FROM MONOPOLY

Remember that it is inefficient when there are potential Pareto improvements. In other words, if an action can be taken where the gains outweigh the losses, and by compensating the losers everyone could be made better off, then there is a deadweight loss. When we move from a monopoly market to a competitive one, market surplus increases by $1.2 billion. This means that the monopoly causes a $1.2 billion deadweight loss.

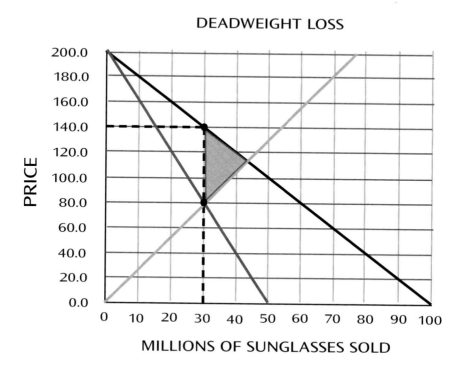

DEADWEIGHT LOSS

PRICE

MILLIONS OF SUNGLASSES SOLD

FIGURE 8.1I

Remember that deadweight loss is only a result in deviations from the equilibrium *quantity*. Between 30 million sunglasses and 42 million sunglasses, consumers are willing to pay more than the firm's marginal cost, so MB >MC. Since the monopolist is unwilling lower its price to increase output (and lose revenue from its pre-existing sales), the deadweight loss persists.

[The shaded] region in Figure 8.1i is a measure of the loss to society from having monopoly rather than competition.

Glossary

Marginal Revenue
the increase in revenue resulting from a marginal increase in quantity

Monopoly
a situation in which one firm produces all of the output in a market

Single-priced Monopoly
a monopolist that can only charge one price

8.2 FIXING MONOPOLY

PRICE DISCRIMINATION

Before looking at how policy can be used to correct a monopoly, let's first consider a simpler solution. In the last section, we introduced a single price monopoly, saying that the monopolist must charge the same price to all consumers. In reality, monopolists tend to practice **price discrimination** meaning they charge a different price to different consumers, with the aim of charging the maximum of each consumer's willingness to pay.

This is seen in practice in many different ways. The most common is price discrimination based on demographics. Discounts for seniors or children who are willing to pay less for the good allow the monopolist to still capture revenue from these consumers. Companies may also create slightly different offerings or brands to appeal to different crowds. Luxottica, for example, sells higher priced Ray-Bans to cater to a more fashion-conscious crowd, and Oakley caters to consumers who care more about functionality. Let's look at how the different price points affect market surplus.

...

In this situation, Luxottica sells sunglasses at two different prices: Ray-Bans at $160 and Oakleys at $120. Notice the effect this has on producer surplus. Whereas at $140 Luxottica sold 30 million units, at the two prices it can sell 40 million, and the average price of the sunglasses is still $140 million. This benefits some consumers who can purchase sunglasses at the lower cost but hurts some who now have to pay a higher price. The deadweight loss has shrunk considerably.

Can we ever remove the deadweight loss entirely? For the producer, this would be preferred as the more it can differentiate prices, the more surplus it receives. Consider a case where the producer can charge the exact willingness to pay of each consumer, a **perfect price discrimination**.

...

[In this case] the deadweight loss has been completely negated, but so has consumer surplus. The monopolist ultimately aims for this situation but is often prohibited from doing so by the difficulty of breaking consumers into segments, government regulation, and more. For a monopoly, we will assume from now on that monopolists can only charge one price.

GOVERNMENT POLICY & MONOPOLY

How can the government correct a monopoly? Remember that to correct the deadweight loss and return to an efficient outcome, we must return Q_E to 42 million sunglasses. This means that we need a policy that will increase quantity. Taxes and price floors, in this case, would decrease quantity, so they will be ineffective. A subsidy would be difficult to implement. Even though it would increase market surplus, it would have the interesting effect of giving the monopolist, who is already charging consumers more that the competitive equilibrium price, more revenue.

This leaves us with a price ceiling, which can be fairly effective in removing deadweight loss. ...

Glossary

Perfect Price Discrimination
the action of selling the same product at a different price to each consumer, equal to their maximum willingness to pay

Price Discrimination
the action of selling the same product at different prices to maximize profits

8.3 WHY MONOPOLIES PERSIST

Because of the lack of competition, monopolies tend to earn significant economic profits. These profits should attract vigorous competition as described in Perfect Competition, and yet, because of one particular characteristic of monopolies, they do not. Barriers to entry are the legal, technological, or market forces that discourage or prevent potential competitors from entering a market. Barriers to entry can range from the simple and easily surmountable, such as the cost of renting retail space, to the extremely restrictive. For example, there are a finite number of radio frequencies available for broadcasting. Once the rights to all of them have been purchased, no new competitors can enter the market.

In some cases, barriers to entry may lead to monopoly. In other cases, they may limit competition to a few firms. Barriers may block entry even if the firm or firms currently in the market are earning profits. Thus, in markets with significant barriers to entry, it is *not* true that abnormally high profits will attract new firms, and that this entry of new firms will eventually cause the price to decline so that surviving firms earn only a normal level of profit in the long run.

There are two types of monopoly, based on the types of barriers to entry they exploit. One is a **natural monopoly**, where the barriers to entry are something other than legal prohibition. The other is a **legal monopoly**, where laws prohibit (or severely limit) competition.

NATURAL MONOPOLY

Economies of scale can combine with the size of the market to limit competition. Figure 8.3a presents a long-run average cost curve for the airplane manufacturing industry. It shows economies of scale up to an output of 8,000 planes per year and a price of P0, then constant returns to scale from 8,000 to 20,000 planes per year, and diseconomies of scale at a quantity of production greater than 20,000 planes per year.

Now consider the market demand curve in the diagram, which intersects the long-run average cost (LRAC) curve at an output level of 6,000 planes per year and at a price P_1, which is higher than P_0. In this situation, the market has room for only one producer. If a second firm attempts to enter the market at a smaller size, say by producing a quantity of 4,000 planes, then its average costs will be higher than the existing firm, and it will be unable to compete. If the second firm attempts to enter the market at a larger size, like **8,000** planes per year, then it could produce at a lower average cost—but it could not sell all 8,000 planes that it produced because of insufficient demand in the market.

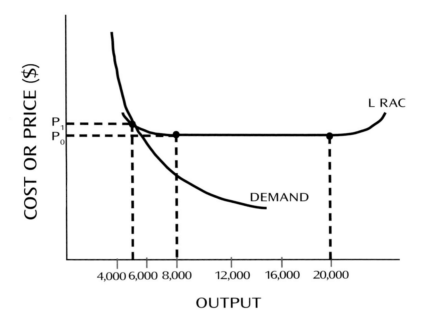

FIGURE 8.3A.

Economies of Scale and Natural Monopoly. In this market, the demand curve intersects the long-run average cost (LRAC) curve at its downward-sloping part. A natural monopoly occurs when the quantity demanded is less than the minimum quantity it takes to be at the bottom of the long-run average cost curve.

   This situation, when economies of scale are large relative to the quantity demanded in the market, is called a natural monopoly. Natural monopolies often arise in industries where the marginal cost of adding an additional customer is very low, once the fixed costs of the overall system are in place. Once the main water pipes are laid through a neighborhood, the marginal cost of providing water service to another home is fairly low. Once electricity lines are installed through a neighborhood, the marginal cost of providing additional electrical service to one more home is very low. It would be costly and duplicative for a second water company to enter the market and invest in a whole second set of main water pipes, or for a second electricity company to enter the market and invest in a whole new set of electrical wires. These industries offer an example where, because of economies of scale, one producer can serve the entire market more efficiently than a number of smaller producers that would need to make duplicate physical capital investments.

A natural monopoly can also arise in smaller local markets for products that are difficult to transport. For example, cement production exhibits economies of scale, and the quantity of cement demanded in a local area may not be much larger than what a single plant can produce. Moreover, the costs of transporting cement over land are high, and so a cement plant in an area without access to water transportation may be a natural monopoly.

CONTROL OF A PHYSICAL RESOURCE

Another type of natural monopoly occurs when a company has control of a scarce physical resource. In the U.S., one historical example of this pattern occurred when the Aluminum Company of America (ALCOA) controlled most of the supply of bauxite, a key mineral used in making aluminum. Back in the 1930s, when ALCOA controlled most of the bauxite, other firms were simply unable to produce enough aluminum to compete.

As another example, the majority of global diamond production is controlled by DeBeers, a multinational company that has mining and production operations in South Africa, Botswana, Namibia, and Canada. It also has exploration activities on four continents, while directing a worldwide distribution network of rough cut diamonds. Though in recent years they have experienced growing competition, their impact on the rough diamond market is still considerable.

LEGAL MONOPOLY

For some products, the government erects barriers to entry by prohibiting or limiting competition. Under U.S. law, no organization but the U.S. Postal Service is legally allowed to deliver first-class mail. Many states or cities have laws or regulations that allow households a choice of only one electric company, one water company, and one company to pick up their garbage. Most legal monopolies are considered utilities — products necessary for everyday life — that are socially beneficial to have. As a consequence, the government allows producers to become regulated monopolies to ensure that an appropriate amount of these products is provided to consumers. Additionally, legal monopolies are often subject to economies of scale, so it makes sense to allow only one provider.

PROMOTING INNOVATION

Innovation takes time and resources to achieve. Suppose a company invests in research and development and finds the cure for the common cold. In this world of near-ubiquitous information, other companies could take the formula, produce the drug, and because they did not incur the costs of research and development (R&D), undercut the price of the company that discovered the drug. Given this possibility, many firms would choose not to invest in R&D, and as a result, the world would have less innovation.

To prevent this from happening, the patent act was created in Canada as a part of the British North America Act in 1869. A **patent** gives the inventor the exclusive legal right to make, use, or sell the invention for a limited time in Canada. The idea is to provide limited monopoly power so that innovative firms can recoup their investment in R&D, but then to allow other firms to produce the product more cheaply once the patent expires.

A **trademark** is an identifying symbol or name for a particular good, like Chevrolet cars, or the Nike "swoosh" that appears on shoes and athletic gear. A firm can renew a trademark over and over again, as long as it remains in active use.

A **copyright**, according to the Canadian Intellectual Property Office, "is the exclusive legal right to produce, reproduce, publish or perform an original literary, artistic, dramatic or musical work. " No one can reproduce, display, or perform a copyrighted work without permission from the author. Copyright protection generally lasts for the life of the author plus 70 years.

Roughly speaking, the patent law covers inventions and copyright protects books, songs, and art. But in certain areas, like the invention of new software, it has been unclear whether patent or copyright protection should apply. There is also a body of law known as **trade secrets**. Even if a company does not have a patent on an invention, competing firms are not allowed to steal its secrets. One famous trade secret is the formula for Coca-Cola, which is not protected under copyright or patent law, but is simply kept secret by the company.

Taken together, this combination of patents, trademarks, copyrights, and trade secret law is called **intellectual property**, because it implies ownership over an idea, concept, or image, not a physical piece of property like a house or a car. Countries around the world have enacted laws to protect intellectual property, although the time periods and exact provisions of such laws vary across countries.

INTIMIDATING POTENTIAL COMPETITION

Businesses have developed a number of schemes for creating barriers to entry by deterring potential competitors from entering the market. One method is known as **predatory pricing**, in which a firm uses the threat of price cuts to discourage competition. Predatory pricing is a violation of antitrust law, but it is difficult to prove.

Consider a large airline that provides most of the flights between two particular cities. A new, small start-up airline decides to offer service between these two cities. The large airline immediately slashes prices on this route so that the new entrant cannot make any money. After the new entrant has gone out of business, the incumbent firm can raise prices again.

After this pattern is repeated once or twice, potential new entrants may decide that it is not wise to try to compete. Small airlines often accuse larger airlines of predatory pricing: in the early 2000s, for example, ValuJet accused Delta of predatory pricing, Frontier accused United, and Reno Air accused Northwest. In 2015, the Justice Department ruled against American Express and Mastercard for imposing restrictions on retailers who encouraged customers to use lower swipe fees on credit transactions.

In some cases, large advertising budgets can also act as a way of discouraging the competition. If the only way to launch a successful new national cola drink is to spend more than the promotional budgets of Coca-Cola and PepsiCo., not too many companies will try. A firmly established brand name can be difficult to dislodge.

SUMMING UP BARRIERS TO ENTRY

Table 8.3a lists the barriers to entry that have been discussed here. This list is not exhaustive since firms have proved to be highly creative in inventing business practices that discourage competition. When barriers to entry exist, perfect competition is no longer a reasonable description of how an industry works. When barriers to entry are high enough, a monopoly can result.

BARRIER TO ENTRY	GOVERNMENT ROLE?	EXAMPLE
Natural monopoly	Government often responds with regulation (or ownership)	Water and electric companies
Control of a physical resource	No	DeBeers for diamonds
Legal monopoly	Yes	Post office, past regulation of airlines and trucking
Patent, trademark, and copyright	Yes, through protection of intellectual property	New drugs or software
Intimidating potential competitors	Somewhat	Predatory pricing; well-known brand names

Table 8.3a Barriers to Entry

KEY CONCEPTS AND SUMMARY

Barriers to entry prevent or discourage competitors from entering the market. These barriers include: economies of scale that lead to natural monopoly, control of a physical resource, legal restrictions on competition, patent, trademark and copyright protection, and practices to intimidate the competition like predatory pricing. Intellectual property refers to the legally guaranteed ownership of an idea, rather than a physical item. The laws that protect intellectual property include patents, copyrights, trademarks, and trade secrets. A natural monopoly arises when economies of scale persist over a large enough range of output that if one firm supplies the entire market, no other firm can enter without facing a cost disadvantage.

Glossary

Barriers to Entry
the legal, technological, or market forces that may discourage or prevent potential competitors from entering a market

Copyright
a form of legal protection to prevent copying, for commercial purposes, original works of authorship, including books and music

Deregulation
removing government controls over setting prices and quantities in certain industries

Intellectual Property
the body of law including patents, trademarks, copyrights, and trade secret laws that protect the right of inventors to produce and sell their inventions

Legal Monopoly
legal prohibitions against competition, such as regulated monopolies and intellectual property protection

Natural Monopoly
economic conditions in the industry, for example, economies of scale or control of a critical resource, that limit effective competition

Patent
a government rule that gives the inventor the exclusive legal right to make, use, or sell the invention for a limited time

Predatory Pricing
when an existing firm uses sharp but temporary price cuts to discourage new competition

Trademark
an identifying symbol or name for a particular good and can only be used by the firm that registered that trademark

Trade Secrets
methods of production kept secret by the producing firm

8.4 MONOPOLISTIC COMPETITION

We have now explored the two sides of the spectrum. In perfect competition, we assume identical products, and in a monopoly, we assume only one product is available.

Monopolistic competition lies in-between. It involves many firms competing against each other, but selling products that are distinctive in some way. Examples include stores that sell different styles of clothing, restaurants or grocery stores that sell different kinds of food and even products like golf balls or beer that may be at least somewhat similar but differ in public perception because of advertising and brand names. Firms producing such products must also compete with other styles, flavours and brand names. The term "monopolistic competition" captures this mixture of mini-monopoly and tough competition.

Who invented the theory of imperfect competition?
The theory of imperfect competition was developed by two economists independently but simultaneously in 1933. The first was Edward Chamberlin of Harvard University, which published *The Economics of Monopolistic Competition*. The second was Joan Robinson of Cambridge University, which published *The Economics of Imperfect Competition*. Robinson subsequently became interested in macroeconomics where she became a prominent Keynesian, and later a post-Keynesian economist.

DIFFERENTIATED PRODUCTS

A firm can try to make its products different from those of its competitors in several ways: physical aspects of the product, selling location, intangible aspects of the product, and perceptions of the product. Products that are distinctive in one of these four ways are called **differentiated products**.

Physical aspects of a product include all the phrases you hear in advertisements: such as an unbreakable bottle, nonstick surface, freezer-to-microwave, non-shrink, extra spicy, newly redesigned for your comfort. The location of a firm can also create a difference between producers. For example, a gas station located at a busy intersection can probably sell more gas than one located on a small side-road. A supplier to an automobile manufacturer may find that it is advantageous to locate near the car factory.

Intangible aspects can differentiate a product, too. Some intangible aspects may be promises like a guarantee of satisfaction or money back, a reputation for high-quality services like free delivery, or a loan to purchase the product. Finally, **product perception** may occur in the minds of the buyers. For example, many people could not tell the difference in taste between common varieties of beer or cigarettes if they were blind-folded, but because of past habits and advertising, they have strong preferences for certain brands. Advertising can play a role in shaping these intangible preferences.

The concept of differentiated products is closely related to the degree of variety that is available. If everyone in the economy wore only blue jeans, ate only white bread, and drank only tap water, then the markets for clothing, food, and drink would be much closer to perfectly competitive. The variety of styles, flavors, locations, and characteristics creates product differentiation and monopolistic competition.

PERCEIVED DEMAND FOR A MONOPOLISTIC COMPETITOR

A monopolistically competitive firm faces a demand for its goods that is between monopoly and perfect competition. Figure 8.4a offers a reminder that the **demand curve** as faced by a perfectly competitive firm is **perfectly elastic** or flat, because the perfectly competitive firm can sell any quantity it wishes at the prevailing **market price**. In contrast, the demand curve, as faced by a monopolist, is the market demand curve, since a monopolist is the only firm in the market, and hence is downward sloping.

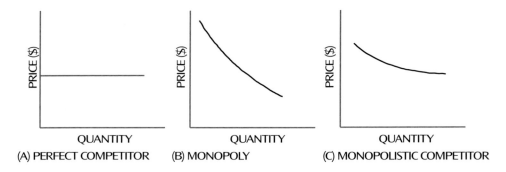

QUANTITY	QUANTITY	QUANTITY
(A) PERFECT COMPETITOR	(B) MONOPOLY	(C) MONOPOLISTIC COMPETITOR

Figure 8.4a. *Perceived Demand for Firms in Different Competitive Settings. The demand curve faced by a perfectly competitive firm is perfectly elastic, meaning it can sell all the output it wishes at the prevailing market price. The demand curve faced by a monopoly is the market demand. It can sell more output only by decreasing the price it charges. The demand curve faced by a monopolistically competitive firm falls in between.*

The demand curve as faced by a monopolistic competitor is not flat, but rather downward-sloping, meaning that the monopolistic competitor, like the monopoly, can raise its price without losing all of its customers or lower its price and gain more customers. Since there are substitutes, the demand curve for a monopolistically competitive firm is relatively more elastic than that of a monopoly, where there are no close substitutes. If a monopolist raises its price, some consumers will choose not to purchase its product—but they will then need to buy a completely different product. However, when a monopolistic competitor raises its price, consumers can choose to buy a similar product from another firm. If a monopolistic competitor raises its price, it will not lose as many customers as would a perfectly competitive firm, but it will lose more customers than a monopoly would.

At a glance, the demand curves faced by a monopoly and monopolistic competitor look similar—that is, they both slope down. Still, the underlying economic meaning of these demand curves is different because a monopolist faces the market demand curve and a monopolistic competitor does not.

Cellular Competition

Recall that monopolistic competition refers to an industry that has more than a few firms that each offer a distinguished product. The Canadian cellular industry is one such market. With a history dating back as far as Alexander Graham Bell's invention of the telephone in 1876, the Canadian cellular industry now has a number of large firms including Rogers, Telus, and Bell. What about Fido, Koodo, and Virgin Mobile? They are owned by Rogers, Telus, and Bell, respectively. While this market has some similarities to an Oligopoly (which we will not explore in this course), it is often classified as a monopolistic competition.

Consider what you would do if your monthly cell phone bill increased by $2. Would you switch to another company? Likely not. This means that the cellular market is certainly not perfectly competitive as cell phone companies have some ability to change prices. Therefore, the demand faced by each of the cellular companies will be more elastic than market demand, but not perfectly elastic. Let's explore how these monopolistic competitive firms set prices.

THE BENEFITS OF VARIETY AND PRODUCT DIFFERENTIATION

Even though monopolistic competition does not provide efficiency, it does have benefits of its own. Product differentiation is based on variety and innovation. Many people would prefer to live in an economy with many kinds of clothes, foods, and car styles; not in a world of perfect competition where everyone will always wear blue jeans and white shirts, eat only spaghetti with plain red sauce, and drive an identical model of car. Many people would prefer to live in an economy where firms are struggling to figure out ways of attracting customers by methods like friendlier service, free delivery, guarantees of quality, variations on existing products, and a better shopping experience.

Economists have struggled, with only partial success, to address the question of whether a market-oriented economy produces the optimal amount of variety. Critics of market-oriented economies argue that society does not really need dozens of different athletic shoes or breakfast cereals or automobiles. They argue that much of the cost of creating such a high degree of product differentiation, and then of advertising and marketing this differentiation, is socially wasteful—that is, most people would be just as happy with a smaller range of **differentiated products** produced and sold at a lower price. Defenders of a market-oriented economy respond that if people do not want to buy differentiated products or highly advertised brand names, no one is forcing them to do so. Moreover, they argue that consumers benefit substantially when firms seek short-term profits by providing differentiated products. This controversy may never be fully resolved, in part because deciding on the optimal amount of variety is very difficult, and in part because the two sides often place different values on what variety means for consumers.

...

How does advertising impact monopolistic competition?

The Canadian economy spent about $12.22 billion on advertising in 2016, according to statista.com.

Advertising is all about explaining to people, or making people believe, that the products of one firm are differentiated from the products of another firm. In the framework of monopolistic competition, there are two ways to conceive how advertising works: either advertising causes a firm's perceived demand curve to become more inelastic (that is, it causes the perceived demand curve to become steeper), or advertising causes demand for the firm's product to increase (that is, it causes the firm's perceived demand curve to shift to the right). In either case, a successful advertising campaign may allow a firm to sell either a greater quantity or to charge a higher price, or both, and thus increase its profits.

However, economists and business owners have also long suspected that much of the advertising may only offset other advertising. Economist A. C. Pigou wrote the following back in 1920 in his book, *The Economics of Welfare*:

> *It may happen that expenditures on advertisement made by competing monopolists [that is, what we now call monopolistic competitors] will simply neutralise one another, and leave the industrial position exactly as it would have been if neither had expended anything. For, clearly, if each of two rivals makes equal efforts to attract the favour of the public away from the other, the total result is the same as it would have been if neither had made any effort at all.*

SUMMARY

Monopolistic competition refers to a market where many firms sell differentiated products. Differentiated products can arise from characteristics of the good or service, location from which the product is sold, intangible aspects of the product, and perceptions of the product.

If the firms in a monopolistically competitive industry are earning economic profits, the industry will attract entry until profits are driven down to zero in the long run. If the firms in a monopolistically competitive industry are suffering economic losses, then the industry will see an exit of firms until economic profits are driven up to zero in the long run.

MARKET TYPE	DESCRIPTION	MR V P	P V MC	LR π	LR ATC	DWL
PERF. COMP	MANY SELLERS, IDENTICAL GOODS, FREE ENTRY IN LR	MR = P	P = MC	π = 0	ATC_{LR} = ATC_{MIN}	NO
MONOPOLY	SINGLE SELLER, BARRIERS TO ENTRY	MR < P	P > MC	π > 0	ATC_{LR} > ATC_{MIN}	YES
MONOPOLISTIC COMP.	MANY SELLERS, DIFFERENTIATED PRODUCTS, FREE ENTRY IN LR	MR < P	P > MC	π = 0	ATC_{LR} > ATC_{MIN}	Y

A monopolistically competitive firm is not efficient because it does not produce at the minimum of its average cost curve or produce where P = MC. Thus, a monopolistically competitive firm will tend to produce a lower quantity at a higher cost and charge a higher price than a perfectly competitive firm.

Monopolistically competitive industries do offer benefits to consumers in the form of greater variety and incentives for improved products and services. There is some controversy over whether a market-oriented economy generates too much variety.

The following table summarizes the three types of market structure we have examined. The fourth, oligopoly, is not in the scope of this course.

Glossary
Differentiated Products
a product that is perceived by consumers as distinctive in some way

Monopolistic Competition
many firms competing to sell similar but differentiated products

1. From an economic standpoint, what are the drawbacks of monopolies?

2. What can be done in order to prevent or reduce the frequency of monopolies?

"EU COMPETITION WATCHDOGS WOULD BE WISE TO WATCH OUT FOR APPLE'S GROWTH," BY ALEKSEJ HEINZE AND EVGENIA KANELLOPOULOU, FROM *THE CONVERSATION*, NOVEMBER 28, 2014

Apple's market value has reached a record-breaking US$700 billion, far outstripping its nearest rival. In a year of superlatives, the company's shares have risen by 60% and it made its largest ever acquisition, paying US$3 billion for Beats Music. But, with Europe voting to break up Google, Apple's growth raises some questions on whether they too could be getting too big and if regulators would want to step in.

Apple follows in the footsteps of Microsoft and Google in a bid to maintain its household name in the constantly evolving digital business landscape. But both Microsoft and Google have learned to their expense that being dominant in their respective markets can attract the attention of the competition authorities, such as the EU Competition Commission.

The European Economic Area is the largest in the world and any global business such as Apple is interested in maximising their international trade in this lucrative market. And, Europe too, with its prioritisation of the digital economy through the development of EU Single Market rules for the digital era under its Digital Agenda is eager to attract global players such as Apple.

But, as Apple looks intent on challenging Spotify's dominance of the music streaming market, with reports that its Beats music service will feature in future versions of Apple's operating system, this could attract competition commission regulators' attention.

The original purchase of Beats was announced in May 2014 and approved by the European Commission (EC) in July, and later by the US regulators. The two product markets that the sale affects are the hardware market for headphones and the market for streaming music.

The headphone market is much simpler than that for streaming. While individuals are easily satisfied with one or two sets of headphones, streaming provides potentially infinite numbers of subscribers and therefore a huge market. This is where the strategic purchase for Apple has the highest potential rewards. Plus, the delivery of an electronic good such as a song has lower overheads compared to the cumbersome packaging and supply chain arrangements needed for shipping and storing a set of headphones.

DOWNLOADS AND STREAMING

At the time of evaluating the competition case of Apple's acquisition of Beats, the EC deemed there to be no need to differentiate between music used for download and music used for streaming. Yet the two are quite different.

Streaming music is a concept where we essentially rent access to songs for a monthly or yearly fee. In music, a similar attitude is developing to that of video – where once you have watched a video film you rarely want to watch it again. Consumers might have their favourites but they are keen to have access to an unlimited number of songs.

When iTunes first came out, it was a revolutionary market place for buying music digitally. Now, however, while it is still profitable, growth is slow. Users are increasingly aware of and opposed to the iTunes licensing models by which even if you pay for music you do not "own" it, rather you are granted a non-exclusive licence to use it. These restrictions and the relative cheapness of streaming has turned public interest towards streaming models instead.

COULD APPLE GET TOO BIG?

If a business dominates a market, breaks have to be applied by the competition regulator to prevent monopolies from controlling the market. In terms of the Apple-Beats case, the EC gave the green light, originally not considering the streaming service an issue since they are only entering the hardware market in Europe.

Although Apple iTunes offered streaming for the US and the Australian market, it was not offered in the EEC. Similarly, Beats Music was only available for the US and Australian market at the time of their merger assessment by the EC. And, should they start streaming in Europe, the assessment considered that Spotify and Deezer users in Europe are sufficient competitors for Apple Beats.

But perhaps the competition assessment fails to take into consideration the overall size of Apple and the price restraints it can potentially pose on its competitors, due to its presence in adjacent markets. Apple has access to more than 800 million Apple IDs – people who can very easily switch to streaming. So, will this mean that Apple Beats is going to dominate the streaming music market? The regulators will certainly be watching this case closely.

1. Although European regulators don't believe Apple has a monopoly on streaming or downloading music, the author questions whether the company has so much power outside of Europe that it could influence competition in the European market. Based on what you know about monopolies so far, do you think this is a valid concern?

2. If Apple doesn't have a monopoly but does have influence over competitors, do you think the government should step in to create more competition? Why or why not?

"AFTER YEARS OF TALK, A REGULATOR IS WILLING TO TAKE ON GOOGLE," BY MARTIN MOORE, FROM *THE CONVERSATION*, APRIL 30, 2015

The European Commission's decision to charge Google with abuse of its dominant market position in the search business in order to favour its own services has been criticised as too narrow in focus, too superficial for not dealing with the bigger problem of digital competition, ill-conceived for messing with the market, or not focused on the real problem of who owns our personal data.

While these are valid criticisms in their own way, they miss the most important point – that legal action has been taken at all. Whatever the result, this is a seismic and seminal move.

The US Federal Trade Commission (FTC) flirted with legal action in 2012 but withdrew, despite the conclusions of an leaked internal investigation that found that Google had "unlawfully maintained its monopoly over general search and search advertising".

The European Commission worked closely with the FTC on its investigation and, like the FTC, decided against launching action by 2013. Joaquin Almunia, head of the European Competition Commission between 2010 and 2014, tried and failed to reach acceptable negotiated settlements with Google on three occasions. But his successor, Margrethe Vestager, has chosen action over discussion.

When the FTC launched an antitrust case against Microsoft in 1998 it dragged on for years, cost the organisation huge amounts of money and effort, and arguably opened up the space for Google to expand and eat much of Microsoft's lunch. As journalist Charles Arthur writes in his book *Digital Wars*, the FTC's action had a devastating impact on Microsoft's self-esteem and "reached into the company's soul".

The case against Microsoft also shows why the FTC and the commission were reticent to launch a case against Google. It was legally and technologically complex, with courts struggling to apply 19th century antitrust law to the digital 21st century. Many people ended up dissatisfied with the result.

HURDLES COULD TRIP UP EITHER SIDE

The case against Google has the potential to be even more complex and legally challenging. To demonstrate Google has abused its dominance the commission may need to call upon economists, engineers, investigative journalists and perhaps even sociologists.

It will need to define the markets in which Google acts. General search may be a relatively established market, but what about vertical search, or social search? It will need to translate competition law to a digital environment, to understand how algorithms work, and the extent to which Google's algorithms favour the company, and to show evidence of abuse. It will also need to establish whether Google's actions have damaged "consumer welfare".

The European Commission will need to do all this while being intensively lobbied by some of the world's largest and most powerful corporations, for example through the Microsoft-sponsored Initiative for a Competitive Online Marketplace (ICOMP).

It's not a great surprise, therefore, that the commission is charging Google on narrow grounds, in this case on favouring its own comparison shopping product. Shopping ought to be relatively low-hanging fruit: a reasonably well-defined market that Google has tried (unsuccessfully) to enter on more than one occasion with previous products Froogle, Google Product Search, and Google Shopping. There are a number of vocal, disgruntled competitors such as Yelp, Expedia and TripAdvisor. And there is evidence upon which to build a case, compiled by the commission and the FTC since 2010.

The commission hopes that by narrowly focusing its action in the first instance it can create a precedent from which to build. It has already signalled where it may go next, having announced a formal investigation into Android, Google's mobile operating system, on the same day. Concerns over Google's web content scraping and its exclusivity agreements with advertising partners have also been highlighted as potential areas of inquiry.

LEGAL RAMIFICATIONS

Whichever way the result falls, the repercussions will be pivotal. If the commission wins it will create a precedent with which the commission may choose to take on the dominance of other digital giants such as Amazon and Facebook. It may also trigger action by other governments and private actions. For Google it could lead to a crisis of confidence and loss of market lead similar to that experienced by Microsoft.

The consequences could be even more significant if the commission loses. Some will see it as evidence of the unchallengeable power of the global tech titans. Some will see it as confirmation that the legal action was merely European anger at US tech success. Few other democratic governments will be likely to take up cudgels and follow the commission's lead.

However, the most likely result is that Google will settle. Though, as has been pointed out in reference to previous attempts to negotiate with the firm Google, settlements could create a precedent too, which could make it difficult in the future to pursue Google for anti-competitive behaviour in one field having settled for the same in another.

In his landmark book The Master Switch, Tim Wu outlined the stages of each information cycle. First a period of openness characterised by innovation, entrepreneurship and relative confusion. Then consolidation, in which a small number of organisations grow dominant. And finally monopolisation of markets – and often subsequent government intervention. For the web, the commission's antitrust action against Google may well signify the start of the final stage of the cycle.

1. As the author notes, it's often difficult for courts and governments to figure out how to regulate digital companies. Why do you think it's so hard for authorities to regulate internet-based businesses?

2. At the time this was written, no government had yet challenged Google's hold on internet searches. Do you think the situation explained in the report constitutes a monopoly?

"AMERICA'S BROADBAND MARKET NEEDS MORE COMPETITION," BY HERNÁN GALPERIN, ANNETTE M. KIM, AND FRANÇOIS BAR, FROM *THE CONVERSATION*, MARCH 5, 2017

The United States is home to some of the most creative people and businesses on the planet. Our filmmakers, artists, software engineers and scientists entertain the world and expand the boundaries of human knowledge. Their creative process is often a mystery, but their tools are not. Among these tools, few are more critical than the internet, which fosters creativity and innovation by facilitating access to information and supporting collaborative work. It is the enzyme that accelerates the creative economy, much like waterways, railroads and roads fueled the industrial era.

But there is a catch: Our world-class creators live in communities where internet access services are far from world-class. Take the example of Los Angeles, a major creativity hub: Using data from the California Public Utilities Commission, we mapped the availability of different home internet services across Los Angeles County. We then combined the results with demographic data, which allowed us to analyze the interplay between internet infrastructure and community demographics in close geographical detail.

Our results show that nearly two-thirds of Angelenos live in areas served by just one internet provider that offers speeds meeting the Federal Communications Commission's current definition of "broadband" service – 25 Mbps download and 3 Mbps upload. Competition is slightly stronger in the wealthier areas of the county, along the coast and in the San Fernando Valley.

Weak competition yields high prices for consumers and little pressure for companies to upgrade their networks to offer better service. For example, in LA County, fiber-based services (capable of delivering speeds far faster than legacy technologies like cable or DSL) are available in less than a quarter of census blocks. By comparison, fiber coverage in cities like Stockholm and Paris (where residents have a choice of at least six providers) is approaching 100 percent. Further, the speeds offered in monopoly areas are 35 percent lower than those offered in areas with three or more competitors. This suggests that increasing competition in America's broadband market would offer a better on-ramp to the creative lifeline of the internet.

LITTLE HEAD-TO-HEAD COMPETITION

The situation in LA County reflects two major trends in U.S. broadband markets:
1) The ongoing industry consolidation in the telecom and cable TV markets;

2) Weak competition between DSL (which uses existing landline telephone wires to deliver broadband) and cable-internet services.

One of our key findings is that there is almost no geographical overlap between competitors with the same technology. Of the more than 73,000 census blocks in LA County – the smallest unit of geography government data can be broken into – only about 2,500 (3 percent) are served by more than one DSL provider. Likewise, only 850 blocks (about 1 percent) are served by more than one cable-internet provider. Alas, most households have to choose between one cable provider and one DSL provider; often, one of them fails to meet the FCC's broadband speed threshold.

Competition has reached such lows that recent mergers aren't making much difference. Take, for example, Charter Communications' acquisition of Time Warner Cable in May 2016, a mega-merger of cable rivals that was expected to reduce competition and increase prices throughout LA County. But fewer than 1 percent of Angelenos lived in areas previously served by both operators. The merger couldn't reduce competition because there was so little to begin with, as companies divvy up territory to avoid competition.

The most recent FCC Broadband Report finds that the situation in Los Angeles is typical of other large metro areas. And it is worse in rural America, where 40 percent of residents lack access to broadband services.

COMMUNITIES STAND UP FOR THEMSELVES

A key barrier to more competition is the expense of installing wired networks across large areas. In the past, federal policies required the few companies with existing networks to allow competing providers to serve customers over those same wires. But those days are gone, largely because the incumbent cable and phone companies successfully fought them in court.

As a result, many local governments have taken matters into their own hands. In 2014, LA Mayor

Eric Garcetti launched CityLinkLA seeking to secure private investments in high-speed internet networks that would provide every resident with a basic level of internet service for free, or at very low cost. The system Garcetti envisioned would also be able to offer much faster speeds than today's commercial service – 1 Gbps or more – at competitive rates.

So far, however, CityLinkLA has not attracted large investments in new broadband infrastructure, particularly for gigabit-speed services. Moreover, our analysis shows that fiber-optic investments have been concentrated in wealthier communities, exacerbating the growing divide between those with lightning-speed home connections and a digital underclass forced to rely on their smartphones and mobile data plans.

Geography and demographics present numerous challenges to the roll-out of advanced network infrastructure in many U.S. cities, including Los Angeles. However, an analysis by the Center for Public Integrity shows that, when comparing US and French cities with similar population densities (such as Nice and Columbus, OH), Americans paid more and had less choice in broadband. If our people and businesses are to continue thriving in a knowledge-based economy, and if we seek to build new opportunities for struggling communities, we must do better.

Help is unlikely to come from Washington, where the newly appointed FCC chairman has consistently voted against federal subsidies for broadband expansion projects. Rather, we should look at the example of communities across America, large and small, that are building upon existing city assets to accelerate the equitable deployment of next-generation internet infrastructure. For example, the city of Los Angeles already owns over 800 miles of fiber optic cable, and there is significant spare capacity. This and other locally owned assets can be leveraged to offer Angelenos, and Americans, the world-class internet service they deserve.

1. The authors discuss some of the problems that can arise from a monopoly on internet access, such as high prices. In your own words, explain why high prices are such a problem.

2. Why do you think poor communities are more hurt by monopolies than wealthier communities?

CHAPTER 2

WHAT THE GOVERNMENT AND POLITICIANS SAY

Although monopolies have always existed, it wasn't until the nineteenth century that it became a problem that required government intervention. Part of that is because prior to the nineteenth century, most businesses operated locally and provided necessary services and goods to citizens, leaving little room for competition. Once it became easier for businesses to expand their service areas, however, there was more competition, and it didn't always benefit the consumer. So governments had to get involved to help small companies remain competitive and keep larger companies from taking advantage of the people. As you read the following articles, you'll have to consider whether government intervention benefits the people or harms businesses, and which outcome is more important.

EXCERPT FROM "DATA CONTROL AND DIGITAL REGULATORY SPACE(S): TOWARDS A NEW EUROPEAN APPROACH," BY ROXANA RADU AND JEAN-MARIE CHENOU, FROM *INTERNET POLICY REVIEW*, JUNE 30, 2015

In November 2010, the European Commission opened an antitrust investigation against Google Inc. based on allegations that the company had abused its dominant position in online search to favour its own services in violation of the EU competition rules. The investigation tried to determine whether Google Inc. had altered the ranking of its algorithm to promote its own services and to 'de-mote' competitors (EU Commission, 2010). Such behaviour would constitute a clear violation of article 102 of the Treaty of the EU that prohibits "any abuse by one or more undertakings of a dominant position within the internal market or in a substantial part of it [...] as incompatible with the internal market in so far as it may affect trade between Member States" (TFEU, 2012, former art. 82 TCE). In this case, the promotion by Google of its own services at the expense of competitors would amount to what is described in the Treaty as "applying dissimilar conditions to equivalent transactions with other trading parties, thereby placing them at a competitive disadvantage" (TFEU, 2012, Art. 102, § c).

After a four-year scrutiny, the European Commission reopened its investigation into Google's search and advertising services. On 15 April 2015, the European Commission sent a Statement of Objections to Google. It contained a number of preliminary conclusions that paved the way to sanctions against the company. It concluded that Google had abused its dominant position in the online search market to favour its own services and in order to divert traffic away from its competitors, as early as 2008. More specifically, the Statement of Objections stresses five points (EU Commission, 2015a): (1) the systematic positioning and prominent display of Google's comparison shopping service in Google's general search results pages, irrespective of its merits; (2) the differentiated application of a system of penalties that 'de-motes' comparison shopping services and that is not applied to Google's own service; (3) the growth in market shares of Google's successive comparison shopping service after the implementation of the changes in the algorithms compared to the poor performance of Froogle, Google's first comparison shopping service that did not benefit from the same algorithmic treatment; (4) the systematic favouring of Google's comparison shopping services after the failure of Froogle; (5) the negative impact of these practices on consumers and innovation.

The preliminary conclusions of the European Commission have triggered a process in which Google Inc. is able to respond to the allegations (until the end of June 2015) and to organise an oral hearing with the Commission. At the end of the process, if the infringement of competition rules is confirmed, the Commission can take a wide array of "appropriate measures to bring it to an end" (TFEU, 2012, art. 105). Moreover, the Commission was put under pressure by the European Parliament that voted a non-binding resolution to break up Google in November 2014. While a break-up of the digital giant is unlikely to be decided, important financial sanctions might be taken against Google. Beyond the financial aspect of the case, the determination of the European institutions to take regulatory measures targeting US internet giants is an important symbolic step towards the creation of a European regulatory space on the internet, also signalled in the Digital Single Market strategy of the European Commission.

It is interesting to note that a similar investigation by the Federal Trade Commission in the US was settled in 2013. As the final report of the FTC states:

> We have not found sufficient evidence that Google manipulates its search algorithms to unfairly disadvantage vertical websites that compete with Google-owned vertical properties. Although at points in time various vertical websites have experienced demotions, we find that this was a consequence of algorithm changes that also could plausibly be viewed as an improvement in the overall quality of Google's search results (FTC, 2013).

The strong reactions by US officials after the EU Parliament's non-binding resolution to break up Google and after the recent move by the EU Commission on the antitrust case illustrate the different perceptions of the situation on the two sides of the Atlantic. US President Obama depicted the EU policies as protectionism:

> We have owned the internet. Our companies have created it, expanded it, perfected it in ways that they can't compete. And often times what is portrayed as high-minded positions on issues sometimes is just designed to carve out some of their commercial interests (Swisher, 2015).

However, the resolution was highly controversial in Europe as well. The decision was depicted as a political move supported by Google competitors rather than a regulatory move. On the other hand, some voices in the US also advocate for a stronger regulation of digital markets. For example, Thomas Rosch, the FTC Commissioner, expressed some dissent about the FTC settlement with Google:

> The Commission's mission is to protect competition and consumers. The proposed "settlement" here will do the opposite. The Commission's acceptance of a commitment letter to resolve an alleged violation of the antitrust laws is an unjustified and dangerous weakening of the Commission's law enforcement authority" (Rosch, 2012).

The debate on both sides of the Atlantic indicates that the recent developments within EU institutions to regulate digital markets and big data controllers represent a struggle between competing norms for the governance of digital markets rather than anti-American protectionism. The antitrust case against Google is only a first step in a wider attempt by the EU in this direction. The alleged unfair promotion of its own services by Google is only one of the four concerns expressed by the EU Commission with regards to Google's practices. While the present antitrust case addresses the way Google displays its search services compared to its competitors, further investigations are to be expected on the Google use of content from other websites; on Google's dominance over advertising on search terms; and on restrictions that surround how advertisers can move their campaigns to other search engines.

A formal investigation has been opened on the possible anti-competitive measures taken by Google concerning its mobile operating system Android. Google allegedly imposed the pre-installation of its services to smartphones and tablet manufacturers, prevented the development and marketing of modified and potentially competing versions of Android, and bundled certain applications to other Google services (EU Commission, 2015b). The following section explores the meaning of the new European approach by combining the analysis of the economic aspects to the societal aspects outlined in the previous section.

TOWARDS A EUROPEAN REGULATORY SPACE ON THE INTERNET

The current growth of digital markets based on e-commerce and the exploitation of big data rests on a set of social institutions that ensure the protection of basic norms for market operation. Their development cannot be disconnected from the promotion of (Western) values that broadly define our understanding of the interplay between public and private actors, such as trust online or the enforcement of intellectual property rules. This reconfigures the roles of organisations and carves out new spaces for regulation (Chenou and Radu, 2015). The laissez-faire approach of the 1990s was believed to create the appropriate conditions for the development of the EU as "the most competitive and dynamic knowl-edge-based economy in the world" (European Council, 2000).

The failure of the Lisbon strategy, despite some successful initiatives such as the '.eu' top-level domain, became obvious. Since 2010, a new approach of the EU towards the governance of digital markets seems to be emerging. Legal and political processes target in particular digital giants with headquarters outside its territory, offering services to European users. More than reacting to the changes brought about by the ubiquitous internet, the European institutions work towards creating a new regulatory space that counters data control as a form of monopolistic power. The value-laden rules that start to be imposed shape the development of digital markets in an unprecedented way. While recognising the dominant position of private intermediaries, the new General Data Protection Regulation and the Digital Single Market strategy represent new means to enhance the EU governance of digital markets and to go beyond a conventional approach.

In defining this regulatory space, instances of contestation over what is to be regulated, while not a new feature in global governance processes (Radu, Chenou & Weber, 2014), probe the boundaries of European institutions. By remaining ambiguous about the implementation of the 'right to be forgotten', the CJEU opened the door for advocating in favour of the global applicability of the decision. Specifically, the CJEU decision triggered debates as to whether the Google practice of removing links from European local versions of the search engine fully protects European citizens' rights. Moreover, a broader inquiry into the e-commerce sector has recently been launched by the European Commission as part of a Digital Single Market strategy tackling issues such as telecommunication regulation, copyright, data protection and IT security. Against this background, the anti-trust case against Google appears to be an element of a broader political project rather than just a circumstantial reaction or a protectionist trend.

What is at stake here goes beyond operating in a more regulated framework. It targets the development of new norms that out-rival the transatlantic divide in key policy areas, including privacy protection and anti-trust sanctioning and seek to establish global rules. Legal scholar Frank Pasquale called for a European digital regulator that would not reproduce the weaknesses of the enforcement of competition rules in digital markets in the US. The two cases analysed in this article show that, in structuring a new approach to governance in the digital age, European institutions proactively work towards the same goal by reconfiguring their own mandates, rather than transferring responsibilities to a new regulator.

1. The European Union (EU) found that Google was in violation of EU rules about competition because of how Google favored its own products in searches. Do you think this is a matter of a monopoly, or do you think a company favoring its own product is an acceptable part of business?

2. After considering the previous question, explain whether you think the rules should be different for digital companies and products than for physical products and services.

"GETTING SERIOUS ABOUT INFORMATION SHARING FOR CYBERSECURITY," BY MICHAEL DANIEL, FROM THE WHITE HOUSE ARCHIVES, APRIL 10, 2014

Our cybersecurity in large part depends on the strength of the weakest part of a network. So, it is critical that the private sector, federal, state and local governments, and communities work together to build up our cyber security. Today's announcement by the Department of Justice and the Federal Trade Commission that they have issued guidance to clarify that cybersecurity information can be shared with competitors without violating antitrust law – long a perceived barrier to effective cybersecurity – is so important. These two agencies, together charged with enforcing our antitrust laws, have made clear today that they do not believe "that antitrust is – or should be – a roadblock to legitimate cybersecurity information sharing."

We know sharing threat information is critical to effective cybersecurity. Indeed, reducing barriers to information sharing is a key element of this Administration's strategy to improve the nation's cybersecurity, and we are aggressively pursuing these efforts through both executive action and legislation. Today's announcement makes clear that when companies identify a threat, they can share information on that threat with other companies and help thwart an attacker's plans across an entire industry.

We know many companies are already sharing information on cyber threats with each other and with the government through programs that preserve the privacy of Americans, maintain appropriate constraints on government access to private information, and do not lead to anti-competitive practices.

For example, during the denial-of-service attacks that targeted the websites of many leading U.S. banks over the last few years, the Financial Services Information Sharing and Analysis Center brought these banks together to exchange information with each other and with the Federal government. That information helped companies manage the attacks.

Non-profit information sharing organizations such as Boston's Advanced Cybersecurity Center, the Bay Area Security Council, and ChicagoFirst have shown value in building smaller trust networks across sectors in metropolitan areas. And many for-profit information sharing organizations are also stepping into the game.

We will continue to work with our partners in industry to encourage the development of a network of information sharing partnerships and to identify actions we can take to further reduce barriers to information sharing.

While the Administration works to expand the sharing of cybersecurity information through executive action, we will work with Congress to carefully update laws to further facilitate cybersecurity information sharing while preserving the rights of individuals. We can and should increase information sharing while working in partnership with companies and organizations to secure their networks and protecting the privacy of their customers.

We also will continue to work to address the concerns our private sector partners have raised that the government should share more of its own information, so that companies could better protect themselves.

Last year, the President's Executive Order on Improving Critical Infrastructure Cybersecurity opened up a Defense Department program created to protect the defense sector to companies across all 16 critical infrastructure sectors of the economy. The program, Enhanced Cybersecurity Services, gives participating commercial security providers access to the classified signatures that are used to protect the government's own networks.

The President also required federal agencies to promptly notify victims or targets of malicious cyber activity. We have already made thousands of such notifications. And we are working to increase the volume, timeliness, and utility of the information we share.

Our goal is for the government to be a reliable information sharing partner, but only one of many. Companies that are targeted by criminals and nation state actors should establish information sharing channels with the National Cybersecurity & Communications Integration Center at the Department of Homeland Security, law enforcement agencies such as the FBI and Secret Service, and with other relevant agencies; however, they should also build information sharing relationships with private sector partners and organizations.

In today's networked world, a cyber threat to one is really a cyber threat to all. This is why steps such as today's announcement by the Department of Justice and the Federal Trade Commission that can encourage more information sharing are key to building up our collective cybersecurity. Companies should assess whether the remaining risks they perceive for engaging in legitimate information sharing are greater than those they face for failing to protect their customer data, their intellectual property, and their business operations from the growing cyber threats to them.

1. To prevent digital monopolies, companies are expected to not collude, or work together, to push out the competition. However, the author suggests that digital companies need to work together for better cybersecurity. Do you think this risks companies working together to create monopolies, too? Explain.

2. Based on what you've read, what are some things that the government can do to help companies share information without creating a monopoly?

"BEYOND ANTITRUST: THE ROLE OF COMPETITION POLICY IN PROMOTING INCLUSIVE GROWTH," BY JASON FURMAN, FROM THE WHITE HOUSE ARCHIVES, SEPTEMBER 16, 2016

[Editor's note: Figures are not included in this reproduction, but can be found with the original article.]

This is an expanded version of these remarks as prepared for delivery.

Thank you very much for inviting me to today's conference. Discussions of competition often center on issues of antitrust enforcement. Those are important issues, but I will not address them in my remarks today because they are enforcement questions that are within the purview of the Antitrust Division of the Justice Department and the Federal Trade Commission (FTC). I will argue, though, that public policy can play an important role in promoting competition that goes well beyond traditional antitrust enforcement.

The Administration has focused on competition policy in a wide range of areas, from airport slots to standards essential patents to spectrum allocation. Most recently, this past April, the President signed an Executive Order calling on agencies to identify creative actions that they can take to promote competition. The Executive Order calls on agencies to maintain a focus on competition policy in the future by submitting proposed actions on a semi-annual basis. The Administration is currently reviewing the first set of proposals from agencies on how we can use public policy to promote competition, a number of which will be announced in the coming months.

The first action undertaken as part of this Executive Order was the Administration filing in support of the Federal Communication Commission's (FCC) proposed rule to bring increased competition to the market for cable set-top boxes. We have been pleased to see FCC Chairman Wheeler actively listen to the many stakeholders involved to improve the proposal, and believe that he is charting out a responsible way to address their meaningful concerns while being responsive to Congress's explicit directive to ensure a healthy set-top marketplace.

In conjunction with the Executive Order, the Council of Economic Advisers (CEA) released an issue brief documenting some of the evidence suggesting a reduction in competition throughout the economy. Our findings are consistent with recent arguments from academic papers such as Bennett and Gartenberg (2016), and other observers, including *The Economist* and the Center for American Progress (CAP), stating that competition in the U.S. economy has declined in recent years (The Economist 2016; Jarsulic et al. 2016).

Part of the underlying motivation for the Administration's effort s is the belief that competition can play an important and broader role not just in static, allocative efficiency but also in dynamic efficiency—making the economy more innovative and increasing productivity growth. In addition, there is also increasing evidence that greater competition or more evenly balanced power in some areas could also play a role in reducing some of the causes of inequality.

In my remarks today, I will start by quickly reviewing some of the evidence for greater concentration in the economy, then provide some broad macroeconomic motivation, before discussing a few specific areas that the Administration is working on, with a focus on some of the difficult questions raised by the rapid evolution of technology in recent years.

WHAT IS THE EVIDENCE ON THE TRENDS IN CONCENTRATION?

The CEA issue brief released earlier this year reviewed some of the evidence on increased concentration in the economy. The majority of industries have seen increases in the revenue share enjoyed by the 50 largest firms between 1997 and 2012 (Table 1). Along similar

TABLE 1

CHANGE IN MARKET CONCENTRATION BY SECTOR, 1997-2012

INDUSTRY	REVENUE EARNED BY 50 LARGEST FIRMS, 2012 (BILLIONS $)	REVENUE SHARE EARNED BY 50 LARGEST FIRMS, 2012	PERCENTAGE POINT CHANGE IN REVENUE SHARE EARNED BY 50 LARGEST FIRMS, 1997-2012
TRANSPORTATION AND WAREHOUSING	307.9	42.1	11.4
RETAIL TRADE	1,555.8	36.9	11.2
FINANCE AND INSURANCE	1,762.7	48.5	9.9
WHOLESALE TRADE	2,183.1	27.6	7.3
REAL ESTATE RENTAL AND LEASING	121.6	24.9	5.4
UTILITIES	367.7	69.1	4.6
EDUCATIONAL SERVICES	12.1	22.7	4.2*
PROFESSIONAL, SCIENTIFIC, AND TECHNICAL SERVICES	278.2	18.8	2.8*
ARTS, ENTERTAINMENT, AND RECREATION	39.5	19.6	2.5*
ADMINISTRATIVE/ SUPPORT	159.2	23.7	1.6
HEALTH CARE AND ASSISTANCE	350.2	17.2	0.8*
ACCOMMODATION AND FOOD SERVICES	149.8	21.2	0.1
OTHER SERVICES, NON-PUBLIC ADMIN	46.7	10.9	- 0.2

lines, *The Economist* (2016) found that in 42 percent of the roughly 900 industries examined, the top four firms control led more than a third of the market in 2012, up from 28 percent of industries in 1997. Of course, an increase in revenue concentration at the national industry level is neither necessary nor sufficient to indicate increases in market power: the sectors listed here are much larger than the relevant markets, whether in terms of sub-sectors or geography, and 50 firms is likely well above the number that would mark an industry as competitive. Nevertheless, it is one metric among many that create a snapshot of the current state of competition in today's economy.

These broad trends are consistent with a number of industry-specific studies tracking concentration over longer periods of time:

- In financial services, a study found that the loan market share of the top ten banks increased from about 30 percent in 1980 to about 50 percent in 2010 (Corbae and D'Erasmo 2013).
- The share of revenues held by the top four firms increased between 1972 and 2002 in eight of nine agricultural industries tracked in a Congressional Research Service study (Shields 2010).
- According to Gaynor, Ho, and Town (2015), hospital market concentration increased from the early 1990s to 2006. The authors found that the average Herfindahl-Hirschman Index (HHI), a commonly used measure of market concentration, increased by about 50 percent to about 3,200, the level associated with just three equal-sized competitors in a market.[1]

- Wireless providers saw increased concentration, with the FCC (2015) finding t hat the average HHI in the markets they examined increased from under 2,500 in 2004 to over 3,000 in 2014.
- Railroad market concentration increases between 1985 and 2007 have been documented by Prater et al. (2012).

While these facts all suggest that concentration has increased, it is also necessary to consider the cause s of that increase in concentration. Our normative evaluation of the policy implications would differ depending on whether this increase is the result of greater economies of scale, or the result of artificial barriers to entry. The causes may also vary from sector to sector or across geographic markets. This is why even though the broader motivation is important, any particular policy issue area should be evaluated on its own merits—which is what I attempt to provide a sampling of below.

SEVEN BROADER MACROECONOMIC TRENDS AND THEIR RELATIONSHIP TO THE COMPETITIVE LANDSCAPE

But before getting to these more specific issues, I want to spend a few moments on some broader macroeconomic trends that are consistent with increased concentration and decreased competition coming specifically from barriers to entry (and in the case of the labor market, barriers to mobility), and on some of their macroeconomic consequences. Let me highlight seven of them:

1. *The economy has seen a slowdown in the creation of new businesses, as the average business is now older and the top firms capture more market share.*

Since the 1980s, young firms (those five years old or less) have been declining as a share of the economy. In 1982, young firms accounted for about half of all firms, and one-fifth of total employment. However, these figures have fallen to about one - third of firms and one - tenth of total employment in 2013 (Figure 1).

Much of this decrease is driven by declining firm dynamism—the entry and exit of firms. While firm exit has been remained relative steady since the late 1970s, the firm entry rate has decreased significantly since the late 1970s (Figure 2).

A partial explanation for the decline in firm entry rates may be found in increased barriers to entry. These barriers to entry can come in the form of advantages that have accrued to incumbents over time. For example, increased economies of scale may mean that incumbents experience lower costs than new firms, making it harder for entrants to compete. Or demand-side network effects—when a product or service increases in quality the more people use it—may tip the scale in favor of a single provider. Incumbent advantages may also come in the form of successful political lobbying, in which incumbent firms have the resources to lobby for rules that pro-tect them from new entrants.

2. *Labor markets have become less fluid, with workers less likely to move between jobs, industries, occupa-tions, and locations.*

Like firm dynamism, labor market dynamism—also known as "fluidity" or "churn, " measured as the frequency of changes in who is working for whom in the labor market—has been declining in recent decades. The causes and consequences of this decline are still not entirely clear: on the one hand, lower levels of churn may suggest better worker-employer matching, but may also be a particular cause for concern given that, for many workers, wage increases typically occur at the point of job-switching (Molloy et al. 2016).

We know relatively more about job flows (job creation and destruction) than worker flows (hires and separations) since series data are available back to the 1980s. Literature based on these data concludes that job flows have markedly declined over the last 20 to 30 years. For example, Decker et al. (2014) and Davis and Haltiwanger (2014) document that job creation and job destruction fell from the late 1980s to just before the 2007 recession, as shown in Figure 3. Hyatt and Spletzer (2013) find larger declines, of roughly one-quarter to one-third, for both job creation and destruction between the late 1990s and 2010.

Although data on worker flows are more recent, they too show evidence of reduced fluidity. There has been a long-run downward trend in job-to-job transitions since at least 2000 (Hyatt and Spletzer 2013). Other measures of worker mobility that extend further back in time also show evidence a steady decline. Long-distance migration in the United States, which typically involves a change of employer or labor force status, has also been in a decades-long decline, falling by as much as 50 percent since the late 1970s

(Molloy et al. 2014; Kaplan and Schulhofer-Wohl 2012). Both intra- and inter- county migration have followed similar patterns, as shown in Figure 4.

While the causes of decreased labor market dynamism are not well understood, research ha s shown that it is related both to changes in firm composition—with employment being increasingly concentrated in older, larger firms—and to declines in worker movements between existing jobs (Davis and Haltiwanger 2014; Hyatt and Spletzer 2013). Both market concentration and frictions that reduce worker mobility can lead to greater monopsony power for employers. With fewer firms competing for a given type of worker, each firm is more likely to exercise local monopsony, and their smaller numbers may also facilitate tacit or explicit collusion. If, on top of that, employees face greater search frictions or costs of moving, then this reduces their ability to raise their wages by changing jobs and thus also reduces their bargaining power with their current employer (Manning 2003).

3. *The share of income going to capital has risen, and the share of income going to labor has fallen.*

Up until recently, the share of income in the nonfarm business sector accruing to labor was generally stable, though it varied somewhat from year to year depending on the economy's cyclical position. This was considered such a strong empirical regularity that it was enshrined in the pantheon of Nicholas Kaldor's stylized facts about growth (Kaldor 1957).

69

But starting around 2000, the distribution of income between labor and capital shifted noticeably away from the former and towards the latter, as shown in Figure 5. Today, the labor share of income is in the mid-50s, compared to the mid-60s two decades ago. A large literature has examined this decline in the labor share of income, and candidate explanations include institutional changes, including the decline of private-sector unions and fall in the real value of the minimum wage; the general reduction in competition shifting the balance of bargaining power towards employers; and skill-biased technological change (Elsby, Hobijn, and Sahin 2013; Karabarbounis and Neiman 2013; Blanchard 1997; Bentolila and Saint-Paul 2003; Azmat, Manning, and van Reenen 2011; Harrison 2005; Jaumotte and Tytell 2007).

4. *The rate of return on capital has risen relative to the safe rate of return.*

Since the 1980s, the safe rate of return, as measured by real interest rates on government bonds, has fallen steadily. However, the rate of return on capital—both all private capital and nonfinancial corporate capital—has held steady or even increased over the same period, mirroring, at least in the last decade and a half, the share of income going to capital instead of to labor (Figure 6).

One explanation of the apparent increase in the premium on the return to capital is that it is another manifestation of the decrease in the labor share of income and associated increase in the capital share of income. This, in turn, is consistent with the increased prevalence of economic rents and a broader trend of reduced competition, although other explanations, including the changing risk characteristics of returns to private capital or government bonds could also be playing a role (Kozlowski, Veldkamp, and Venkateswaran 2015; Campbell, Pflueger, and Viceira 2014).

5. But businesses are investing less.

Contrary to what economic theory would predict, the higher returns to capital have not been associated with an increase in business investment. In fact, business investment has been particularly weak in recent years. Some of most recent weakness likely represents temporary adjustments to transitory factors, like low oil prices, but nonresidential fixed investment as a share of overall GDP has shown a downward trend since the 1980s, as shown in Figure 7. Again, multiple explanations are possible. One explanation is that monopoly power has increased—which is consistent with higher returns and lower output.

Low levels of business investment are particularly troubling because of their impact on productivity growth via capital deepening. The largest contributor to recent low productivity growth has been the decline, for the first time since World War II, in capital services per worker-hour in the last five years—due to both slower investment growth and a large increase in worker hours. As a result, a worker today has less capital at his or her disposal than a worker five years ago.

6. *The rate of return across businesses has become increasingly dispersed.*

Recent years have also seen dramatic increases in the dispersion of returns to firms, as returns on invested capital for publicly-traded U.S. nonfinancial firms have become increasingly concentrated. Figure 8 indicates that the 90th percentile firm sees returns on investment in capital that are more than five times the median. The ratio was closer to two just a quarter of a century ago.

This concentration of returns among a small number of firms raises the question of whether, and to what extent, economic rents may be playing a role here, too. The data show that two-thirds of the non-financial firms enjoying an average return on invested capital of 45 percent or higher between 2010 and 2014 were in either the health care or information technology sectors, industries where, as mentioned above, other measures point to a reduction in competition (Furman and Orszag 2015).

7. *Wage inequality has grown substantially between workers at different businesses and establishments.*

As is often noted, income inequality has increased in the United States over the last several decades. Recent research from Song et al. 2016 suggests that especially among firms with 100 to 1,000 employees (which contain over 70 percent of employees and 99 percent of firms), a large share of this inequality is driven by increased divergence in the average earnings of workers in *between* different firms rather than a divergence of the wages *within* the same firm. This finding is consistent with evidence from Barth et al. (2014) on establishments. Figures 9a and 9c show that while individual wage disparities have clearly risen, so too have disparities among firms. Figure 9 b, which shows the individual wage structure divided by the firm wage structure, demonstrates that between-firm changes account for much of the increased dispersion in individual wages. These trends could indicate that a prime driver of inequality is the difference between the most and least profitable companies, although it also may reflect the sorting of workers with different abilities across firms—the subject of a long-standing debate over inter-industry wage differentials (Krueger and Summers 1988; Katz 1992; Abowed et al. 2012).

These seven trends are not concrete proof of decreased competition stemming from barriers to entry, but that is one explanation consistent with the facts I have presented. Declining firm dynamism, high returns and low output, and disparities in the rate of return on investment are all potential consequences of increasing barriers to entry.

SOME PRO-COMPETITION POLICY APPLICATIONS

To the extent that these macroeconomic trends are related to decreased competition, then pro-competitive policies have potential to not only benefit consumers but also improve the state of the macroeconomy by, for example, increasing productivity and ensuring that the benefits of growth are widely shared. For these reasons, the Administration has taken several significant policy actions to promote competition. I will next briefly touch on four examples.

INTELLECTUAL PROPERTY AND PATENT REFORM

The first area I will discuss is in some senses the intellectually and substantively hardest: intellectual property and patent reform. In this case, of course, intellectual property protections are intended to increase innovation by granting temporary monopoly power—increasing the private rate of return to investments in research that might otherwise have been competed away. But it has also long been understood that a balance needs to be struck between the dynamic incentives conferred by intellectual property and the static costs of the monopoly power, a balance that is manifested in the finite lives and limited scope of patents, trademarks and copyrights. Moreover, it is increasingly understood that overly stringent intellectual property practices can impede innovation itself—including by reducing the follow-on innovation that so often can be important, especially in areas like technology.

These considerations have played a role in the Administration's approach to patent policy. For example, many of the interconnected services available today require different firms to use the same standard technology. The Administration recognized that if that technology was patented, the patent holder could exercise excessive power and "hold up" the ecosystem over a "standards essential patent" that was necessary for increasingly interconnected devices to work together. In response to this, the U.S. Patent and Trade Office and DOJ came together to provide guidance to the International Trade Commission (ITC) and suggest ways to prevent that hold up—guidance that was the basis for the President's decision to block the ITC's exclusion order on certain smartphones based on a claim that they had infringed a standards essential patent.

A second example of the Administration's patent policy is its work to boost patent quality and limit the ability of overly aggressive patent assertion entities to quell innovation. In 2011 the America Invents Act put in place new mechanisms for post-grant review of patents and other re forms to boost patent quality. Further, to hasten the patent litigation process, accused infringers have the opportunity to challenge the patentability of a claim through an *inter partes* review, which is handled by the Patent Trial and Appeal Board rather than a Federal court (which handles the appeals process). This process for challenging the validity of a patent provides a quick, inexpensive alternative to district court litigation, and should help improve patent quality and ultimately reduce frivolous litigation.

INCREASING THE BARGAINING POWER OF WORKERS

Generally, it is a goal of economic policy to increase competition and then let the market discover prices. In some markets, however, some monopoly or monopsony power is inevitable. In the case of monopsony, the labor market is one leading and important example because search costs and other labor market frictions make it hard for employees to shop around for another employer any time they experience changes in their wages or job conditions. Considerations like commuting costs, which tie employees to their current employers, give those employers some power to set the parameters of pay negotiations or even pay lower wages .

There is no reason to think incentives to exercise market power are any less powerful in the labor market than they are in the product market. Even as far back as Adam Smith (1776) economists have noted that:

> What are the common wages of labor, depends everywhere upon the contract usually made between [employers and employees], whose interests are by no means the same. The workmen desire to get as much, the masters to give as little as possible. The former are disposed to combine in order to raise, the latter in order to lower the wages of labor. It is not, however, difficult to foresee which of the two parties must, upon all ordinary occasions, have the advantage in the dispute, and force the other into a compliance with their terms. The masters, being fewer in number, can combine much more easily...

As this quote suggests, employers can more easily dictate the level of wages and other terms of employment when they are few in numbers—and this is a potential concern with the rising concentration of the U.S. markets. (However, since explicit and illegal wage collusion is a matter under the purview of enforcement agencies, I will not discuss such issues further.)

However, employers can also shift the balance of power in their favor by means that are legal in many States, including through the increasingly widespread practice of non-compete agreements. By reducing workers' job options, non-compete agreements force workers to accept lower wages in their current jobs, and may sometimes induce workers to leave their occupations entirely, foregoing accumulated human capital (U.S.

Treasury 2015). By one estimate, 18 percent of those in the U.S. labor force, or roughly 28 million people, are currently covered by non-compete agreements (Star, Bishara, and Prescott 2016). While such agreements can sometimes promote innovation through the protection of trade secrets, they are common among workers who are less likely to possess such secrets, especially lower-skilled workers (U. S. Treasury 2015).

Other frictions that reduce worker mobility and increase monopsony power can occur naturally. These include the costs of moving, commuting, and searching for another job. And labor market frictions can also be created by restrictions such as occupational licensing laws and overly stringent land-use policies that drive up housing costs. Regardless of the source, such frictions effectively reduce competition among firms in the market for labor. With fewer competitors, employers are able to pay lower wages, and they have an incentive to do so— even if this means reducing employment and forgoing some productive employment relationships.

While enforcement can and does play a role in promoting competition in labor markets, some market power is inevitable and policy should concern itself with how this power is balanced. Traditionally, monopsony power in labor markets was countered in the United States by two institutions—unions and minimum wage laws. An important benefit was distributional: both unions and minimum wages helped bolster the wages of lower- and middle-wage workers and, in turn, helped reduced inequality. But to the extent that they helped to counter monopsony power, they also helped to limit inefficiently low employment that results when firms pay sub-competitive wages.

But union membership has declined consistently since the 1970s, as shown in Figure 10. Approximately a quarter of all U.S. workers belonged to a union in 1955 but, by 2015, union membership had dropped to just below 10 percent of total employment, roughly the same level as the mid-1930s. In some states, just 3 percent of workers belong to unions (CEA 2015).

At the same time, the real value of the minimum wage has declined 24 percent since its peak of $9.55 in 1968 (Figure 11), eroding its ability to protect those workers with the fewest options and the least bargaining power.

REFORMING OCCUPATIONAL LICENSING

One example of policies that create inefficient and inequitable rents is the requirement of a government-issued license to be employed in certain professions ("occupational licensing"). The share of the U.S. workforce covered by State licensing laws grew five-fold in the second half of the 20th century, from less than 5 percent in the early 1950s to 25 percent by 2008, as shown in Figure 12 (Kleiner and Krueger 2013). While licensing can play an important role in protecting consumer health and safety, there is evidence that some licensing requirements create economic rents for licensed practitioners at the expense of excluded workers and consumers—increasing inefficiency and potentially also increasing inequality (Furman 2015).

Not only have licensing laws proliferated in recent years, they also vary dramatically across States. The patchwork of State regulations and the lack of reciprocity agreements has raised the cost of moving across State lines for workers in licensed occupations, and may be one factor contributing to the decline in geographic mobility (Department of the Treasury, Office of Economic Policy, Council of Economic Advisers, and Department of Labor 2015).

In 2015, the Administration released a series of best practices to help State and local governments better tailor their occupational licensing laws to meet consumer health and safety needs without acting as undue barriers to entries into particular occupations. And this summer, the Department of Labor invested $7.5 million to support States' efforts to increase the portability of licenses across State lines and to lower barriers to enter the labor market through reforming licensure. Since the release of the best practices and recommendations last year, legislators in at least 11 States have proposed 15 reforms in line with these recommendations, and four State bills have passed so far.

REFORMING LAND-USE REGULATION

Competition policy also has applications beyond traditional product or labor markets. One such area is in the housing and land sectors. Nationwide, real house prices have grown substantially faster than real construction costs since at least the mid-1980s, implying that returns to scarcity—i.e., "rents" in the economic sense—have played an important role in house prices, reducing the stock of affordable housing (Gyourko and Molloy 2015).

Numerous studies, including Glaeser and Gyourko (2003) and Gyourko and Molloy (2015) have argued that land-use regulations are what explain these occurrences of prices that substantially exceed construction costs. As with occupational licensing, well-designed land-use restrictions can play an important role in promoting social welfare. Environmental reasons may make it appropriate to limit high-density or multi-use development in some localities. Similarly, health and safety concerns—such as an area's air traffic patterns, viability of its water supply, or its geologic stability—may merit height and lot size restrictions.

But in a number of cases, overly burdensome land-use restrictions—like minimum lot sizes, off-street parking requirements, height limits, prohibitions on multi-family housing, or lengthy permitting processes—can instead artificially reduce competition by acting as supply constraints. In doing so, such policies both allow a small number of landowners to capture economic rents and reduce the stock of available affordable housing. These constrains can also limit productivity growth and labor mobility by making it more difficult for workers to move to higher-productivity cities (Furman 2015).

Moreover, inappropriate land-use policies can also reduce equity by allowing a small number of individuals to enjoy the benefits of living in a community while excluding many others, limiting diversity and economic mobility. This is of particular concern given recent research by Chetty et al. (2014) showing that economic mobility varies greatly across cities. Moreover, moving from a low to a high mobility area confers lifelong socio-economic benefits on the children whose families move (Chetty at al. 2015).

While most land-use regulations are appropriately made at the State and, especially, the local level, the Federal government can also play a role in encouraging land-use regulations that help, and do not hinder, mobility and economic growth. This month, the Administration will release a new toolkit that highlights actions that States and local jurisdictions are taking to promote affordable, high-opportunity housing markets. These best practices— including streamlining permitting processes, eliminating off-street parking requirements, reducing minimum lot sizes, and enacting high-density and multifamily zoning policies—provide a starting point for other local efforts to reduce overly burdensome land-use policies.

THE FUTURE OF COMPETITION IN THE DIGITAL AGE

One topic we have been grappling with in a range of economic issue areas, including competition policy, is the ever-increasing role that digitization plays in our economy. The digital age has the potential to increase competition in many ways, but at the same time, changing technology will bring new challenges to policymakers, challenges that will come increasingly to the fore as the digital economy expands.

So far, internet markets have tended to favor digital giants that hold high market shares, a characteristic that is traditionally associated with low competition in brick-and - mortar markets. However, understanding the competitive implications of these new markets requires a closer analysis. The markets of the digital economy are in many ways different from "old economy" markets. Some of those differences are differences of degree— the internet lowers many costs for small businesses, increasing their ability to rapidly and inexpensively scale up, collect information on potential consumers, and create new products and ideas. These differences do not transform the structure of the market; instead, they merely lower the cost of doing business. Other differences, however, are differences of type: business models may be dramatically different due to digitization. These differences of type warrant closer consideration.

One type of business model that has flourished with digitization is the "platform" model, which relies heavily on network effects to grow because the primary product is access to other customers. Examples include payment platforms like Pay Pal, sales platforms like eBay, and social networks like Facebook. Switching costs for customers are particularly high in these markets—no one wants to be the first and only user of a platform—and these network effects can act as a barrier to entry.

However, it is not as clear whether these "quasi-monopolies" pose the same harm to consumers as traditional monopolies. In these markets, highly concentrated market share might not be as detrimental to customers as in traditional markets because the services provided by these businesses are more valuable to consumers as their consumer base grows. This means that determining the optimal level of competition in these new markets is a dramatically different and harder task.

Even the task of measuring competition is complicated in digital markets. Usually, economists use prices as indicators of the level of competition, but we cannot necessarily do that here because many markets are two-sided and there are different types of consumer harm. Businesses on the internet are often complementary, so companies may subsidize one side of the market by profiting from the other side of the market. For example, social media sites often offer free services to users and charge for ads. However, the lack of high prices for consumers does not mean that consumer harms or other risks could not occur. Industry watchers have raised concerns about whether the large companies that dominate search and social networking may be able to acquire inefficient power in ads or control people's access to news. Another concern is that instead of raising prices or reducing quantity, these companies may reduce innovation. Firms holding quasi-monopolies may lose the incentive to keep improving the quality of their products.

Switching costs are traditionally an indicator of competition, and many may assume that switching costs in internet markets are virtually zero because competition is just a click away. This may have been true in the early ages of the internet, but to automatically assume zero switching costs now would be to miss a large part of what is happening. For example, the original search engines were merely directories of websites, and their quality didn't depend on how many users they had. However, search engines today collect data on the behavior of their users and use it to improve their services and tailor those services to individual users. Thus, in order for other firms to be competitive, they need a large user base and the data that comes with it. Furthermore, for each individual user looking to switch services, the incumbent, with its existing knowledge of that user, has a significant advantage over a competitor that does not yet know the user and therefore cannot tailor services to him or her.

Lastly, digitization could bring a new level of opacity to businesses. Traditionally, price fixing and collusion could be detected in the communications between businesses. The task of detecting undesirable price behavior becomes more difficult with the use of increasingly complex algorithms for setting prices. This type of a logarithmic price setting can lead to undesirable price behavior, sometimes even unintentionally. The use of advanced machine learning algorithms to set prices and adapt product functionality would further increase opacity.

Competition policy in the digital age brings with it new challenges for policymakers. It will be imperative that agencies continue the great work and creative solutions that came out of the President's Executive Order to promote competition and inclusive growth in the digital age.

CONCLUSION

Recent trends in concentration in a range of industries suggest decreasing levels of competition, and many concerning macroeconomic trends seem to suggest that this decrease not just due to increases in economies of scale, but rather that increases in barriers to entry are playing a role. For the sake of both consumers and the macroeconomy as a whole, the Administration has used and will continue to use public policy to address these concerns. Increasing competition has the potential to drive faster productivity and output growth, faster real wage growth, and increased equity. We have moved forward in areas such as intellectual property and patent reform, increasing worker bargaining power, and reforming occupational licensing and land use regulations. While these are examples of positive changes, our work in promoting competition does not end here. The President's Executive Order will continue to encourage agencies to develop creative solutions for increasing competition by soliciting new ideas on a regular basis. In considering the future of competition policy, we must also keep in mind the way in which changes in the economy, such as digitization, will affect how we evaluate competition effectively.

1. The remarks you just read pose a question: Are these new digital quasi-monopolies as dangerous to consumers as traditional monopolies? Based on what you've learned so far, how would you answer that question?

2. What are some digital businesses that you think, based on what you've read, would qualify as monopolies? Explain.

"EXECUTIVE ORDER—STEPS TO INCREASE COMPETITION AND BETTER INFORM CONSUMERS AND WORKERS TO SUPPORT CONTINUED GROWTH OF THE AMERICAN ECONOMY," BY BARACK OBAMA, FROM THE WHITE HOUSE ARCHIVES, APRIL 15, 2016

By the authority vested in me as President by the Constitution and the laws of the United States of America, and in order to protect American consumers and workers and encourage competition in the U.S. economy, it is hereby ordered as follows:

Section 1. Policy. Maintaining, encouraging, and supporting a fair, efficient, and competitive marketplace is a cornerstone of the American economy. Consumers and workers need both competitive markets and information to make informed choices.

Certain business practices such as unlawful collusion, illegal bid rigging, price fixing, and wage setting, as well as anticompetitive exclusionary conduct and mergers stifle competition and erode the foundation of America's economic vitality. The immediate results of such conduct -- higher prices and poorer service for customers, less innovation, fewer new businesses being launched, and reduced opportunities for workers -- can impact Americans in every walk of life.

Competitive markets also help advance national priorities, such as the delivery of affordable health care, energy independence, and improved access to fast and affordable broadband. Competitive markets also promote economic growth, which creates opportunity for American workers and encourages entrepreneurs to start innovative companies that create jobs.

The Department of Justice (DOJ) and the Federal Trade Commission (FTC) have a proven record of detecting and stopping anticompetitive conduct and challenging mergers and acquisitions that threaten to consolidate markets and reduce competition.

Promoting competitive markets and ensuring that consumers and workers have access to the information needed to make informed choices must be a shared priority across the Federal Government. Executive departments and agencies can contribute to these goals through, among other things, pro-competitive rulemaking and regulations, and by eliminating regulations that create barriers to or limit competition. Such Government-wide action is essential to ensuring that consumers, workers, startups, small businesses, and farms reap the full benefits of competitive markets.

Sec. 2. Agency Responsibilities. (a) Executive departments and agencies with authorities that could be used to enhance competition (agencies) shall, where consistent with other laws, use those authorities to promote competition, arm consumers and workers with the information they need to make informed choices, and eliminate regulations that restrict competition without corresponding benefits to the American public.

(b) Agencies shall identify specific actions that they can take in their areas of responsibility to build upon efforts to detect abuses such as price fixing, anti-competitive behavior in labor and other input markets, exclusionary conduct, and blocking access to critical resources that are needed for competitive entry. Behaviors that appear to violate our antitrust laws should be referred to antitrust enforcers at DOJ and the FTC. Such a referral shall not preclude further action by the referring agency against that behavior under that agency's relevant statutory authority.

(c) Agencies shall also identify specific actions that they can take in their areas of responsibility to address undue burdens on competition. As permitted by law, agencies shall consult with other interested parties to identify ways that the agency can promote competition through pro-competitive rulemaking and regulations, by providing consumers and workers with information they need to make informed choices, and by eliminating regulations that restrict competition without corresponding benefits to the American public.

(d) Not later than 30 days from the date of this order, agencies shall submit to the Director of the National Economic Council an initial list of (1) actions each agency can potentially take to promote more competitive markets; (2) any specific practices, such as blocking access to critical resources, that potentially restrict meaningful consumer or worker choice or unduly stifle new market entrants, along with any actions the agency can potentially take to address those practices; and (3) any relevant authorities and tools potentially available to enhance competition or make information more widely available for consumers and workers.

(e) Not later than 60 days from the date of this order, agencies shall report to the President, through the Director of the National Economic Council, recommendations on agency-specific actions that eliminate barriers to competition, promote greater competition, and improve consumer access to information needed to make informed purchasing decisions. Such recommendations shall include a list of priority actions, including rulemakings, as well as timelines for completing those actions.

(f) Subsequently, agencies shall report semi-annually to the President, through the Director of the National Economic Council, on additional actions that they plan to undertake to promote greater competition.

(g) Sections 2(d), 2(e), and 2(f) of this order do not require reporting of information related to law enforcement policy and activities.

Sec. 3. General Provisions. (a) This order shall be implemented consistent with applicable law and subject to the availability of appropriations.

(b) Independent agencies are strongly encouraged to comply with the requirements of this order.

(c) Nothing in this order shall be construed to impair or otherwise affect:

(i) the authority granted by law to a department or agency, or the head thereof; or

(ii) the functions of the Director of the Office of Management and Budget relating to budgetary, administrative, or legislative proposals.

(d) This order is not intended to, and does not, create any right or benefit, substantive or procedural, enforceable at law or in equity by any party against the United States, its departments, agencies, or entities, its officers, employees, or agents, or any other person.

1. In his executive order, President Obama writes that competitive business measures are good for helping advance national priorities, like economic growth. How does fighting monopolies help the economy?

2. How does promoting competition between businesses help American workers?

CHAPTER 3

WHAT THE COURTS SAY

The courts have yet to catch up to the quickly advancing digital landscape. Technology and the internet have grown and advanced rapidly in the twenty-first century, and laws are typically slow to adapt. The speed with which the internet and computer advancements have allowed things to change has caused the courts to have an even harder time catching up with the way businesses operate in the digital world. The cases that have come before the nation's highest courts regarding digital monopolies have been few and far between, but they are helping to lay the groundwork for future digital antitrust cases.

UNITED STATES V. APPLE, INC., BY CIRCUIT JUDGE DEBRA ANN LIVINGSTON, 2ND US CIRCUIT COURT OF APPEALS, JUNE 30, 2015

DEBRA ANN LIVINGSTON, *Circuit Judge*:

Since the invention of the printing press, the distribution of books has involved a fundamentally consistent process: compose a manuscript, print and bind it into physical volumes, and then ship and sell the volumes to the public. In late 2007, Amazon.com, Inc. ("Amazon") introduced the Kindle, a portable device that carries digital copies of books, known as "ebooks." This innovation had the potential to change the centuries–old process for producing books by eliminating the need to print, bind, ship, and store them. Amazon began to popularize the new way to read, and encouraged consumers to buy the Kindle by offering desirable books — new releases and *New York Times* bestsellers — for $9.99. Publishing companies, which have traditionally stood at the center of the multi-billion dollar book-producing industry, saw Amazon's ebooks, and particularly its $9.99 pricing, as a threat to their way of doing business.

By November 2009, Apple, Inc. ("Apple") had plans to release a new tablet computer, the iPad. Executives at the company saw an opportunity to sell ebooks on the iPad by creating a virtual marketplace on the device, which came to be known as the "iBookstore." Working within a tight timeframe, Apple went directly into negotiations with six of the major publishing companies in the United States. In two months, it announced that five of those companies — Hachette, Harpercollins, Macmillan, Penguin, and Simon & Schuster (collectively, the "Publisher

Defendants") — had agreed to sell ebooks on the iPad under arrangements whereby the publishers had the authority to set prices, and could set the prices of new releases and *New York Times* bestsellers as high as 13 $19.99 and $14.99, respectively. Each of these agreements, by virtue of its terms, resulted in each Publisher Defendant receiving less per ebook sold via Apple as opposed to Amazon, even given the higher consumer prices. Just a few months after the iBook-store opened, however, every one of the Publisher Defendants had taken control over pricing from Amazon and had raised the prices on many of their ebooks, most notably new releases and bestsellers.

The United States Department of Justice ("DOJ" or "Justice Department") and 33 states and territories (collectively, "Plaintiffs") filed suit in the United States District Court for the Southern District of New York, alleging that Apple, in launching the iBookstore, had conspired with the Publisher Defendants to raise prices across the nascent ebook market. This agreement, they argued, violated § 1 of the Sherman Antitrust Act, 15 U.S.C. § 1 *et seq.* ("Sherman Act"), and state antitrust laws. All five Publisher Defendants settled and signed consent decrees, which prohibited them, for a period, from restricting ebook retailers' ability to set prices. Then, after a three-week bench trial, the district court (Cote, J.) concluded that, in order to induce the Publisher Defendants to participate in the iBookstore and to avoid the necessity of itself competing with Amazon over the retail price of ebooks, Apple orchestrated a conspiracy among the Publisher Defendants to raise the price of ebooks — particularly new releases and *New York Times* best-sellers. *United States v. Apple Inc.*, 952 F. Supp. 2d 638,

15 647 (S.D.N.Y. 2013). The district court found that the agreement constituted a *per se* violation of the Sherman Act and, in the alternative, unreasonably restrained trade under the rule of reason. See *id.* at 694. On September 5, 2013, the district court entered final judgment on the liability finding and issued an injunctive order that, *inter alia*, prevents Apple from entering into agreements with the Publisher Defendants that restrict its ability to set, alter, or reduce the price of ebooks, and requires Apple to apply the same terms and conditions to ebook applications sold on its devices as it does to other applications.

On appeal, Apple contends that the district court's liability finding was erroneous and that the provisions of the injunction related to its pricing authority and ebook applications are not necessary to protect the public. Two of the Publisher Defendants — Macmillan and Simon & Schuster — join the appeal, arguing that the portion of the injunction related to Apple's pricing authority either unlawfully modifies their consent decrees or should be judicially estopped. We conclude that the district court's decision that Apple orchestrated a horizontal conspiracy among the Publisher Defendants to raise ebook prices is amply supported and well-reasoned, and that the agreement unreasonably restrained trade in violation of § 1 of the Sherman Act. We also conclude that the district court's injunction is lawful and consistent with preventing future anticompetitive harms.

Significantly, the dissent *agrees* that Apple intentionally organized a conspiracy among the Publisher Defendants to raise ebook prices. Nonetheless, it contends that Apple was entitled to do so because the conspiracy helped it become an ebook retailer. In arriving at this star-

tling conclusion — based in large measure on an argument that Apple itself did not assert — the dissent makes
two fundamental errors. The first is to insist that the vertical
organizer of a horizontal price-fixing conspiracy may escape
application of the per se rule. This conclusion is based on a
misreading of Supreme Court precedent, which establishes
precisely the opposite. The dissent fails to apprehend that
the Sherman Act outlaws *agreements* that unreasonably
restrain trade and therefore requires evaluating the nature
of the restraint, rather than the identity of each party who
joins in to impose it, in determining whether the *per se* rule
is properly invoked. Finally (and most fundamentally) the
dissent's conclusion rests on an erroneous premise: that
one who organizes a horizontal price-fixing conspiracy
— the "supreme evil of antitrust," *Verizon Commc'ns Inc.
v. Law Offices of Curtis V. Trinko, LLP*, 540 U.S. 398, 408
(2004) — among those competing at a different level of the
market has somehow done less damage to competition than
its co-conspirators.

The dissent's second error is to assume, in effect,
that Apple was entitled to enter the ebook retail market on
its own terms, even if these terms could be achieved only
via its orchestration of and entry into a price-fixing agreement with the Publisher Defendants. The dissent tells a
story of Apple organizing this price-fixing conspiracy to
rescue ebook retailers from a monopolist with insurmount-
able retail power. But this tale is not spun from any factual
findings of the district court. And the dissent's armchair
analysis wrongly treats the number of ebook retailers at
any moment in the emergence of a new and transforma-
tive technology for book distribution as the sine qua non
of competition in the market for trade ebooks.

More fundamentally, the dissent's theory — that the presence of a strong competitor justifies a horizontal price-fixing conspiracy — endorses a concept of marketplace vigilantism that is wholly foreign to the antitrust laws. By organizing a price-fixing conspiracy, Apple found an easy path to opening its iBookstore, but it did so by ensuring that market-wide ebook prices would rise to a level that it, and the Publisher Defendants, had jointly agreed upon. Plainly, competition is not served by permitting a market entrant to *eliminate price competition* as a condition of entry, and it is cold comfort to consumers that they gained a new ebook retailer at the expense of passing control over all ebook prices to a cartel of book publishers — publishers who, with Apple's help, collectively agreed on a new pricing model precisely to raise the price of ebooks and thus protect their profit margins and their very existence in the marketplace in the face of the admittedly strong headwinds created by the new technology. Because we conclude that the district court did not err in deciding that Apple violated § 1 of the Sherman Act, and because we also conclude that the district court's injunction was lawful and consistent with preventing future anticompetitive harms, we affirm.

BACKGROUND

I. FACTUAL BACKGROUND[1]

We begin not with Kindles and iPads, but with printed "trade books," which are "general interest fiction and non-fiction" books intended for a broad readership. *Apple*, 952 F.Supp.2d

95

at 648 n. 4. In the United States, the six largest publishers of trade books, known in the publishing world as the "Big Six," are Hachette, HarperCollins, Macmillan, Penguin, Random House, and Simon & Schuster. Together, the Big Six publish many of the biggest names in fiction and non-fiction; during 2010, their titles accounted for over 90% of the *New York Times* bestsellers in the United States. *Id.* at 648 n. 5.

For decades, trade book publishers operated under a fairly consistent business model. When a new book was ready for release to the public, the publisher would sell hardcover copies to retailers at a "wholesale" price and recommend resale to consumers at a markup, known as the "list" price. After the hardcover spent enough time on the shelves—often a year—publishers would release a paperback copy at lower "list" and "wholesale" prices. In theory, devoted readers would pay the higher hardcover price to read the book when it first came out, while more casual fans would wait for the paperback.

A. AMAZON'S KINDLE

On November 19, 2007, Amazon released the Kindle: a portable electronic device that allows consumers to purchase, download, and read ebooks. At the time, there was only one other ereader available in the emerging ebook market, and Amazon's Kindle quickly gained traction. In 2007, ebook revenue in North America was only $70 million, a tiny amount relative to the approximately $30 billion market for physical trade books. The market was growing, however; in 2008 ebook revenue was roughly $140 million and, by the time Barnes & Noble, Inc. (Barnes & Noble) launched its Nook ereader in November 2009, Amazon was responsible for 90% of all ebook sales. *Apple*, 952 F.Supp.2d at 648–49.

Amazon followed a "wholesale" business model similar to the one used with print books: publishers recommended a digital list price and received a wholesale price for each ebook that Amazon sold. In exchange, Amazon could sell the publishers' ebooks on the Kindle and determine the retail price. At least early on, publishers tended to recommend a digital list price that was about 20% lower than the print list price to reflect the fact that, with an ebook, there is no cost for printing, storing, packaging, shipping, or returning the books.

Where Amazon departed from the publishers' traditional business model was in the sale of new releases and *New York Times* bestsellers. Rather than selling more expensive versions of these books upon initial release (as publishers encouraged by producing hardcover books before paperback copies), Amazon set the Kindle price at one, stable figure—$9.99. At this price, Amazon was selling "certain" new releases and bestsellers at a price that "roughly matched," or was slightly lower than, the wholesale price it paid to the publishers. *Apple*, 952 F.Supp.2d at 649. David Naggar, a Vice President in charge of Amazon's Kindle content, described this as a "classic loss-leading strategy" designed to encourage consumers to adopt the Kindle by discounting new releases and *New York Times* bestsellers and selling other ebooks without the discount. J.A. 1485. The district court also referred to this as a "loss leader[ ]" strategy, *Apple*, 952 F.Supp.2d at 650, 657, 708, and explained that Amazon "believed [the $9.99] pricing would have long-term benefits for its consumers," *id.* at 649. Contrary to the dissent's portrayal of the opinion, the district court did *not* find that Amazon used the $9.99 price point to "assure [ ] its domination" in the ebook market, or that its pricing strategy acted as a "barrier to entry" for other retailers. Dissenting Op. at 6–7. Indeed, in November 2009—just a few months before Apple's launch of the iBookstore—Barnes & Noble entered the ebook retail market by launching the Nook, Apple, 952 F.Supp.2d at 649 n. 6, and as early as 2007 Google Inc. ("Google") had been planning to enter the market using a wholesale model, *id.* at 686.

B. THE PUBLISHERS' REACTIONS

Despite the small number of ebook sales compared to the overall market for trade books, top executives in the Big Six saw Amazon's $9.99 pricing strategy as a threat to their established way of doing business. Those executives included: Hachette and Hachette Livre Chief Executive Officers ("CEOs") David Young and Arnaud Nourry; HarperCollins CEO Brian Murray; Macmillan CEO John Sargent; Penguin USA CEO David Shanks; Random House Chief Operating Officer Madeline McIntosh; and Simon & Schuster President and CEO Carolyn Reidy. In the short term, these members of the Big Six thought that Amazon's lower-priced ebooks would make it more difficult for them to sell hardcover copies of new releases, "which were often priced," as the district court noted, "at thirty dollars or more," *Apple*, 952 F.Supp.2d at 649, as well as *New York Times* bestsellers. Further down the road, the publishers feared that consumers would become accustomed to the uniform $9.99 price point for these ebooks, permanently driving down the price they could charge for print versions of the books. Moreover, if Amazon became powerful enough, it could demand lower wholesale prices from the Big Six or allow authors to publish directly with Amazon, cutting out the publishers entirely. As Hachette's Young put it, the idea of the "wretched $9 .99 price point becoming a de facto standard" for ebooks "sickened" him. J.A. 289.

The executives of the Big Six also recognized that their problem was a collective one. Thus, an August 2009 Penguin strategy report (concluded only a few months before Apple commenced its efforts to launch the iBook- store) noted that "[c]ompetition for the attention of readers will be most intense from digital companies whose objec- tive may be to [cut out] traditional publishers altogether. It will not be possible for any individual publisher to mount an effective response, because of both the resources neces- sary and the risk of retribution, so the industry needs to develop a common strategy." J.A. 287. Similarly, Reidy from Simon & Schuster opined in September 2009 that the publishers had "no chance of success in getting Amazon to change its pricing practices" unless they acted with a "crit- ical mass," and expressed the "need to gather more troops and ammunition" before implementing a move against Amazon. J.A. 290 (internal quotation marks omitted).

Conveniently, the Big Six operated in a close-knit industry and had no qualms communicating about the need to act together. As the district court found (based on the Publisher Defendants' own testimony), "[o]n a fairly regular basis, roughly once a quarter, the CEOs of the [Big Six] held dinners in the private dining rooms of New York restaurants, without counsel or assistants present, in order to discuss the common challenges they faced." *Apple*, 952 F.Supp.2d at 651. Because they "did not compete with each other on price," but over authors and agents, the publishers "felt no hesitation in freely discussing Amazon's prices with each

other and their joint strategies for raising those prices."
Id. Those strategies included eliminating the discounted wholesale price for ebooks and possibly creating an alternative ebook platform.

The most significant attack that the publishers considered and then undertook, however, was to withhold new and bestselling books from Amazon until the hardcover version had spent several months in stores, a practice known as "windowing." Members of the Big Six both kept one another abreast of their plans to window, and actively pushed others toward the strategy.[2] By December 2009, the *Wall Street Journal* and *New York Times* were reporting that four of the Big Six had announced plans to delay ebook releases until after the print release, and the two holdouts—Penguin and Random House—faced pressure from their peers.

Ultimately, however, the publishers viewed even this strategy to save their business model as self-destructive. Employees inside the publishing companies noted that windowing encouraged piracy, punished ebook consumers, and harmed long-term sales. One author wrote to Sargent in December 2009 that the "old model has to change" and that it would be better to "embrace e-books," publish them at the same time as the hardcovers, "and pray to God they both sell like crazy." J.A. 325. Sargent agreed, but expressed the hope that ebooks could eventually be sold for between $12.95 and $14.95. "The question is," he mused, "how to get there?" J.A. 325.

C. APPLE'S ENTRY INTO THE EBOOK MARKET

Apple is one of the world's most innovative and successful technology companies. Its hardware sells worldwide and supports major software marketplaces like iTunes and the App Store. But in 2009, Apple lacked a dedicated marketplace for ebooks or a hardware device that could offer an outstanding reading experience. The pending release of the iPad, which Apple intended to announce on January 27, 2010, promised to solve that hardware deficiency.

Eddy Cue, Apple's Senior Vice President of Internet Software and Services and the director of Apple's digital content stores, saw the opportunity for an ebook marketplace on the iPad. By February 2009, Cue and two colleagues—Kevin Saul and Keith Moerer—had researched the ebook market and concluded that it was poised for rapid expansion in 2010 and beyond. While Amazon had an estimated 90% market share in trade ebooks, Cue believed that Apple could become a powerful player in the market in large part because consumers would be able to do many tasks on the iPad, and would not want to carry a separate Kindle for reading alone. In an email to Apple's then-CEO, Steve Jobs, he discussed the possibility of Amazon selling ebooks through an application on the iPad, but felt that "it would be very easy for [Apple] to compete with and trounce Amazon by opening up our own ebook store" because "[t]he book publishers would do almost anything for [Apple] to get into the ebook business." J.A. 282.

Jobs approved Cue's plan for an ebook marketplace—which came to be known as the iBookstore—in November 2009. Although the iPad would go to market with or without the iBookstore, Apple hoped to announce the ebook marketplace at the January 27, 2010 iPad launch to "ensure maximum consumer exposure" and add another "dramatic component" to the event. *Apple*, 952 F.Supp.2d at 655. This left Cue and his team only two months amidst the holiday season both to create a business model for the iBookstore and to assemble a group of publishers to participate. Cue also had personal reasons to work quickly. He knew that Jobs was seriously ill, and that, by making the iBookstore a success, he could help Jobs achieve a longstanding goal of creating a device that provides a superior reading experience.

Operating under a tight timeframe, Cue, Saul, and Moerer streamlined their efforts by focusing on the Big Six publishers. They began by arming themselves with some important information about the state of affairs within the publishing industry. In particular, they learned that the publishers feared that Amazon's pricing model could change their industry, that several publishers had engaged in simultaneous windowing efforts to thwart Amazon, and that the industry as a whole was in a state of turmoil. "Apple understood," as the district court put it, "that the Publishers wanted to pressure Amazon to raise the $9.99 price point for e-books, that the Publishers were searching for ways to do that, and that they were willing to coordinate their efforts to achieve that goal." *Id.* at 656. For its part, as the district court found, Apple was willing to sell ebooks at higher prices, but "had decided that it would not open the iBookstore if it could not make money on the store and compete effectively with Amazon." *Id.*

D. APPLE'S NEGOTIATIONS WITH THE PUBLISHERS

1. INITIAL MEETINGS

Apple held its first meetings with each of the Big Six between December 15 and 16. The meetings quickly confirmed Cue's suspicions about the industry. As he wrote to Jobs after speaking with three of the publishers, "[c]learly, the biggest issue is new release pricing" and "Amazon is definitely not liked much because of selling below cost for NYT Best Sellers." J.A. 326–27. Many publishers also emphasized that they were searching for a strategy to regain control over pricing. Apple informed each of the Big Six that it was negotiating with the other major publishers, that it hoped to begin selling ebooks within the next 90 days, and that it was seeking a critical mass of participants in the iBookstore and would launch only if successful in reaching this goal. Apple informed the publishers that it did not believe the iBookstore would succeed unless publishers agreed both not to window books and to sell ebooks at a discount relative to their physical counterparts. Apple noted that ebook prices in the iBookstore needed to be comparable to those on the Kindle, expressing the view, as Reidy recorded, that it could not "tolerate a market where the product is sold significantly more cheaply elsewhere." *Apple*, 952 F.Supp.2d at 657 (internal quotation marks omitted). Most importantly for the publishers, however, Cue's team also expressed Apple's belief that Amazon's $9.99 price point was not ingrained in consumers' minds, and that Apple could sell new releases and *New York Times* bestsellers for somewhere between $12.99 and $14.99. In return, Apple requested that the publishers decrease their wholesale prices so that the company could make a small profit on each sale.

These meetings spurred a flurry of communications reporting on the "[t]errific news[,]" as Reidy put it in an email to Leslie Moonves, her superior at parent company CBS Corporation ("CBS"), that Apple "was not interested in a low price point for digital books" and didn't want "Amazon's $9.95 [sic] to continue." *Apple*, 952 F.Supp.2d at 658 (first alteration in original) (internal quotation marks omitted). Significantly, these communications included numerous exchanges *between* executives at different Big Six publishers who, the district court found, "hashed over their meetings with Apple with one another." *Id.* The district court found that the frequent telephone calls among the Publisher Defendants during the period of their negotiations with Apple "represented a departure from the ordinary pattern of calls among them." *Id.* at 655 n. 14.

2. THE AGENCY MODEL

Meanwhile, Cue, Moerer, and Saul returned to Apple's headquarters to develop a business model for the iBook-store. Although the team was optimistic about the initial meetings, they remained concerned about whether the publishers would reduce wholesale prices on new releases and bestsellers by a large enough margin to allow Apple to offer competitive prices and still make a profit. One strategy that the team considered was to ask publishers for a 25% wholesale discount on all of these titles, so if a physical book sold at $12 wholesale (the going rate for the majority of *New York Times* bestsellers) Apple could purchase the ebook version for $9 and offer it on the iBookstore at a small markup. But Cue was aware that some publishers had increased Amazon's digital whole-sale prices in 2009 in an unsuccessful effort to convince Amazon to change its pricing. *Id.* at 650; J.A. 1771. Cue felt it would be difficult to negotiate wholesale prices down far enough "for [Apple] to generally compete profitably with Amazon's below-cost pricing on the most popular e-books." J.A. 1772. As Cue saw it, Apple's most valuable bargaining chip came from the fact that the publishers were desperate "for an alternative to Amazon's pricing policies and excited about the prospect that [Apple's] entry [into the ebook market] would give them leverage in their negotiations with Amazon." *Apple*, 952 F.Supp.2d at 659.

It was at this point that Cue's team, recognizing its opportunity, abandoned the wholesale business model for a new, agency model.[3] Unlike a wholesale model, in an agency relationship the *publisher* sets the price that consumers will pay for each ebook. Then, rather than the retailer paying the publisher for each ebook that it sells, the publisher pays the retailer a fixed percentage of each sale. In essence, the retailer receives a commission for distributing the publisher's ebooks. Under the system Apple devised, publishers would have the freedom to set ebook prices in the iBookstore, and would keep 70% of each sale. The remaining 30% would go to Apple as a commission.

This switch to an agency model obviated Apple's concerns about negotiating wholesale prices with the Big Six while ensuring that Apple profited on every sale. It did not, however, solve all of the company's problems. Because the agency model handed the publishers control over pricing, it created the risk that the Big Six would sell ebooks in the iBookstore at far higher prices than Kindle's $9.99 offering. If the prices were too high, Apple could be left with a brand new marketplace brimming with titles, but devoid of customers.

To solve this pricing problem, Cue's team initially devised two strategies. First, they realized that they could maintain "realistic prices" by establishing price caps for different types of books. J.A. 359. Of course, these caps would need to be *higher* than Amazon's $9.99 price point, or Apple would face the same difficult price negotiations that it sought to avoid by switching away from the whole-sale model. But at this point Apple was not content to open its iBookstore offering prices higher than the competition. For as the district court found, if the Publisher Defendants "wanted to end Amazon's $9.99 pricing," Apple similarly desired "that there be no price competition at the retail level." *Apple*, 952 F.Supp.2d at 647.

Apple next concluded, then, as the district court found, that "[t]o ensure that the iBookstore would be competitive at higher prices, Apple needed to eliminate all retail price competition." *Id.* at 659. Thus, rather than simply agreeing to price caps above Amazon's $9.99 price point, Apple created a second requirement: publishers must switch all of their other ebook retailers—including Amazon—to an agency pricing model. The result would be that Apple would not need to compete with Amazon on price, and publishers would be able to eliminate Amazon's $9.99 pricing. Or, as Cue would later describe the plan to executives at Simon & Schuster, Macmillan, and Random House, the plan "solve[d][the] Amazon issue" by allowing the publishers to wrest control over pricing from Amazon.[4] *Id.* at 661 (internal quotation marks omitted).

On January 4 and 5, Apple sent essentially identical emails to each member of the Big Six to explain its agency model proposal. Each email described the commission split between Apple and the publishers and recom-mended three price caps: $14.99 for hardcover books with list prices above $35; $12.99 for hardcover books with list prices below $35; and $9.99 for all other trade books. The emails also explained that, "to sell ebooks at realistic prices all [other] resellers of new titles need to be in [the] agency model" as well. J.A. 360. Or, as Cue told Reidy, "all publishers" would need to move "all retailers" to an agency model. J.A.2060.

3. THE "MOST–FAVORED–NATION" CLAUSE

Cue's thoughts on the agency model continued to evolve after the emails on January 4 and 5. Most significantly, Saul—Cue's in-house counsel—devised an alternative to explicitly requiring publishers to switch other retailers to agency. This alternative involved the use of a "most-favored nation" clause ("MFN Clause" or "MFN"). In general, an MFN Clause is a contractual provision that requires one party to give the other the best terms that it makes available to any competitor. In the context of Apple's negotiations, the MFN Clause mandated that, "[i]f, for any particular New Release in hardcover format, the ... Customer Price [in the iBookstore] at any time is or becomes higher than a customer price offered by any other reseller…, then [the] Publisher shall designate a new, lower Customer Price [in the iBookstore] to meet such lower [customer price]." J.A. 559. Put differently, the MFN would require the publisher to offer any ebook in Apple's iBookstore for no more than what the same ebook was offered elsewhere, such as from Amazon.

On January 11, Apple sent each of the Big Six a proposed eBook Agency Distribution Agreement (the "Contracts"). As described in the January 4 and 5 emails, these Contracts would split the proceeds from each ebook sale between the publisher and Apple, with the publisher receiving 70%, and would set price caps on ebooks at $14.99,

$12.99, and $9.99 depending on the book's hardcover price. But unlike the initial emails, the Contracts contained MFN Clauses in place of the requirement that publishers move all other retailers to an agency model. Apple then assured each member of the Big Six that it was being offered the same terms as the others.

The Big Six understood the economic incentives that the MFN Clause created. Suppose a new hardcover release sells at a list price of $25, and a wholesale price of $12.50. With Amazon, the publishers had been receiving the wholesale price (or a slightly lower digital wholesale price) for every ebook copy of the volume sold on Kindle, even if Amazon ultimately sold the ebook for less than that wholesale price. Under Apple's initial agency model—with price caps but no MFN Clause—the publishers already stood to make less money per ebook with Apple. Because Apple capped the ebook price of a $25 hardcover at $12.99 and took 30% of that price, publishers could only expect to make $8.75 per sale. But what the publishers sacrificed in short-term revenue, they hoped to gain in long-term stability by acquiring more control over pricing and, accordingly, the ability to protect their hardcover sales.

The MFN Clause changed the situation by making it imperative, not merely desirable, that the publishers wrest control over pricing from ebook retailers generally. Under the MFN, if Amazon stayed at a wholesale model and continued to sell ebooks at $9.99, the publishers would be forced to sell in the iBookstore, too, at that same $9.99 price point. The result would be the worst of both worlds: lower short-term revenue and no control over pricing. The publishers recognized that, as a practical matter, this meant that the MFN Clause would force them to move Amazon to an agency relationship. As Reidy put it, her company would need to move all its other ebook retailers to agency "unless we wanted to make even less money" in this growing market. Apple, 952 F.Supp.2d at 666 (internal quotation marks omitted). This situation also gave each of the publishers a stake in Apple's quest to have a critical mass of publishers join the iBookstore because, "[w]hile no one Publisher could effect an industry-wide shift in prices or change the public's perception of a book's value, if they moved together they could." *Id.* at 665; *see also* J.A.1981.

Apple understood this dynamic as well. As the district court found, "Apple did not change its thinking" when it replaced the explicit requirement that the publishers move other retailers to an agency model with the MFN. Indeed, in the following weeks, Apple assiduously worked to make sure that the shift to agency occurred. *Apple*, 952 F.Supp.2d at 663. But Apple also understood that, as Cue bluntly put it, "any decent MFN forces the model" away from wholesale and to agency. *Id.* (internal quotation marks omitted). Or as the district court found, "the MFN protected Apple from retail price competition as it punished a Publisher if it failed to impose agency terms on other e-tailers." *Id.* at 665.

Thus, the terms of the negotiation between Apple and the publishers became clear: Apple wanted quick and successful entry into the ebook market and to eliminate retail price competition with Amazon. In exchange, it offered the publishers an opportunity "to confront Amazon as one of an organized group ... united in an effort to eradicate the $9.99 price point." *Id.* at 664. Both sides needed a critical mass of publishers to achieve their goals. The MFN played a pivotal role in this quid pro quo by "stiffen[ing] the spines of the [publishers] to ensure that they would demand new terms from Amazon," and protecting Apple from retail price competition. *Id.* at 665.

4. FINAL NEGOTIATIONS

The proposed Contracts sparked intense negotiations as Cue's team raced to assemble enough publishers to announce the iBookstore by January 27. The publishers' first volley was to push back on Apple's price caps, which they recognized would become the "standard across the industry" for pricing.[5] J.A. 571. In a set of meetings between January 13 and 14, the majority of the Big Six expressed a general willingness to adopt an agency model, but refused to do so with the price limits Apple demanded. Cue responded by asking Jobs for permission to create a more lenient price cap system. Under this new regime, *New York Times* bestsellers could sell for $14.99 if the hardcover was listed above $30, and for $12.99 if listed below that price. As for new releases, a $12.99 cap would apply to hardcovers priced between $25 and $27.50; a $14.99 cap would apply to hardcovers selling for up to $30; and, if the hardcover sold for over $30, publishers could sell the ebook for between $16.99 and $19.99. Jobs responded that he could "live with" the pricing "as long as [the publishers] move Amazon to the agen[cy] model too." J.A. 499.

Cue proposed this new pricing regime to the Big Six on January 16 and, with only 11 days remaining before the iPad launch, turned up the pressure. In each email conveying the new prices, Cue reminded the publishers that, if they did not agree to the iBookstore by the 27th, other companies, including Amazon and Barnes & Noble, would certainly build their own book store apps for the iPad. Correspondence from within the publishing companies also shows that Cue promoted the proposal as the "best chance for publishers to challenge the 9.99 price point," and emphasized that Apple would "not move forward with the store [unless] 5 of the 6 [major publishers] signed the agreement." J.A. 522–23. As Cue said at trial, he attempted to "assure [the publishers] that they weren't going to be alone, so that [he] would take the fear awa[y] of the Amazon retribution that they were all afraid of." J.A.2068 (internal quotation marks omitted). "The Apple team reminded the Publishers," as the district court found, "that this was a rare opportunity for them to achieve control over pricing." *Apple*, 952 F.Supp.2d at 664.

By January 22, two publishers—Simon & Schuster and Hachette—had verbally committed to join the iBookstore, while a third, Penguin, had agreed to Apple's terms in principle. As for the others, Cue was frustrated that they kept "chickening out" because of the "dramatic business change" that Apple was proposing. J.A. 547. To make matters worse, "[p]ress reports on January 18 and 19 alerted the publishing world and Amazon to the Publishers' negotiations with Apple," *Apple*, 952 F.Supp.2d at 670–71, and Amazon learned from Random House that it was facing "pressure from other publishers to move to [the] agency model because Apple had made it clear that unless all of the Big Six participated, they wouldn't bother with building a bookstore," J.A. 1520. Representatives from Amazon descended on New York for a set of long-scheduled meetings with the publishers. As the district court found, "[i]n separate conversations on January 20 and over the next few days, the Publisher Defendants all told Amazon that they wanted to change to an agency distribution model with Amazon." *Apple*, 952 F.Supp.2d at 672.

Macmillan, however, presented an issue for Apple. The district court found that at a January 20 lunch between John Sargent and Amazon, Sargent "announced that Macmillan was planning to offer Amazon the option to choose either an agency [or wholesale] model." *Id.* But at dinner with Cue that night, according to the district court, Cue made sure that Sargent understood the consequences of the MFN, explaining "that Macmillan had no choice but to move Amazon to an agency model if it wanted to sign an agency agreement with Apple."[6] *Id.* The next day, Sargent emailed Cue to express his continued reservations about switching Macmillan's other retailers to an agency relationship.

With the iPad launch fast approaching, Cue enlisted the help of others. Cue had received an email from Simon & Schuster's Carolyn Reidy, who had already verbally committed to Apple's terms and whom Cue would later call the "real leader of the book industry," moments after hearing from Sargent. J.A. 621. Cue then spoke with Reidy for twenty minutes before reaching out to Brian Murray, who, as the district court found, "was fully supportive of the requirement that all e-tailers be moved to an agency model." *Apple*, 952 F.Supp.2d at 673 n. 39. After the discussions, Cue asked Sargent to speak with both Reidy and Murray. Sargent complied, and "spoke to both Murray and Reidy by telephone for eight and fifteen minutes, respectively." *Id.* at 673. Minutes later, Sargent called the Amazon representative to inform him that Macmillan planned to sign an agreement that "required" the company to conduct business with Amazon through an agency model. *Id*. By January 23, Macmillan had verbally agreed to join the iBookstore.

Cue followed a similar strategy with Penguin. While Penguin's CEO David Shanks agreed to Apple's terms on January 22, he informed Cue that he would join the iBookstore only if four other publishers agreed to participate. By January 25, Apple had signatures from three publishers but Penguin was still noncommittal. Cue called Shanks, and the two spoke for twenty minutes. "Less than an hour [later], Shanks called Reidy to discuss Penguin's status in its negotiations with Apple." *Id*. at 675. Penguin signed the Contract that afternoon.

HarperCollins was the fifth, and final, publisher to agree in principle to Apple's proposal. Murray, its CEO, "remained unhappy over the size of Apple's commission and the existence of price caps." Id. at 673 n. 39. Unable to negotiate successfully with Murray, Cue asked Jobs to contact James Murdoch, the CEO of the publisher's parent company, and "tell him we have 3 signed so there is no leap of faith here." *Id*. at 675 (internal quotation marks omitted). After a series of emails, Jobs summarized Apple's position to Murdoch:

> [W]e simply don't think the ebook market can be successful with pricing higher than $12.99 or $14.99. Heck, Amazon is selling these books at $9.99, and who knows, maybe they are right and we will fail even at $12.99. But we're willing to try at the prices we've proposed. As I see it, [HarperCollins] has the following choices: (1) Throw in with [A]pple and see if we can all make a go of this to create a real

mainstream ebooks market at $12.99 and $14.99. (2) Keep going with Amazon at $9.99. You will make a bit more money in the short term, but in the medium term Amazon will tell you they will be paying you 70% of $9.99. They have shareholders too. (3) Hold back your books from Amazon. Without a way for customers to buy your ebooks, they will steal them.

Id. at 677. Cue also emailed Murray to inform him that four other publishers had signed their agreements. Murray then called executives at both Hachette and Macmillan before agreeing to Apple's terms.

As the district court found, during the period in January during which Apple concluded its agreements with the Publisher Defendants, "Apple kept the Publisher Defendants apprised about who was in and how many were on board."[7] *Id.* at 673. The Publisher Defendants also kept in close communication. As the district court noted, "[i]n the critical negotiation period, over the three days between January 19 and 21, Murray, Reidy, Shanks, Young, and Sargeant called one another 34 times, with 27 calls exchanged on January 21 alone." *Id.* at 674.

By the January 27 iPad launch, five of the Big Six— Hachette, HarperCollins, Macmillan, Penguin, and Simon & Schuster—had agreed to participate in the iBookstore. The lone holdout, Random House, did not join because its executives believed it would fare better under a wholesale pricing model and were unwilling to make a complete switch to agency pricing. Steve Jobs announced the iBookstore as part of his presentation introducing the iPad. When asked after the presentation why someone should purchase an ebook from Apple for $14.99 as opposed to $9.99 with Amazon or Barnes & Noble, Jobs confidently replied, "[t]hat won't be the case ... the price will be the same ... [P]ublishers will actually withhold their [e]books from Amazon ... because they are not happy with the price."[8] A day later, Jobs told his biographer the publishers' position with Amazon: "[y]ou're going to sign an agency contract or we're not going to give you the books." J.A. 891 (internal quotation marks omitted).

E. NEGOTIATIONS WITH AMAZON

Jobs's boast proved to be prophetic. While the Publisher Defendants were signing Apple's Contracts, they were also informing Amazon that they planned on changing the terms of their agreements with it to an agency model. However, their move against Amazon began in earnest on January 28, the day after the iPad launch. That afternoon, John Sargent flew to Seattle to deliver an ultimatum on behalf of Macmillan: that Amazon would switch its ebook sales agreement with Macmillan to an agency model or suffer a seven-month delay in its receipt of Macmillan's new releases.[9] Amazon responded by removing the option to purchase Macmillan's print and ebook titles from its website.

Sargent, as the district court found, had informed Cue of his intention to confront Amazon before ever leaving for Seattle.[10] *Apple*, 952 F.Supp.2d at 678. On his return, he emailed Cue to inform him about Amazon's decision to remove Macmillan ebooks from Kindle, adding a note to say that he wanted to "make sure you are in the loop." J.A. 640. Sargent also wrote a public letter to Macmillan's authors and agents, describing the Amazon negotiations. Hachette's Arnaud Nourry emailed the CEO of Macmillan's parent company to express his "personal support" for Macmillan's actions and to "ensure [him] that [he was] not going to find [his] company alone in the battle." J.A. 643. A Penguin executive wrote to express similar support for Macmillan's position.

The district court found that while Amazon was "opposed to adoption of the agency model and did not want to cede pricing authority to the Publishers," it knew that it could not prevail in this position against five of the Big Six. *Apple*, 952 F.Supp.2d at 671, 680. When Amazon told Macmillan that it would be willing to negotiate agency terms, Sargent sent Cue an email titled "URGENT!!" that read: "Hi Eddy, I am gonna need to figure out our final agency terms of sale tonight. Can you call me please?" J.A. 642. Cue and Sargent spoke that night and, while Cue denied at trial that the conversation concerned Macmillan's negotiations with Amazon, the district court found that "his denial was not credible."[11] *Apple*, 952 F.Supp.2d at 681 n. 52. By February 5, Amazon had agreed to agency terms with Macmillan.

The other publishers who had joined the iBookstore quickly followed Macmillan's lead. On February 11, Reidy wrote to the head of CBS that Simon & Schuster was beginning agency negotiations with Amazon. She informed him that she was trying to "delay" negotiations because it was "imperative ... that the other publishers with whom Apple has announced deals push for resolution on their term changes" at the same time, "thus not leaving us out there alone." J.A. 701. Each of the Publisher Defendants then informed Amazon that they were under tight deadlines to negotiate new agency agreements, and kept one another informed about the details of their negotiations. As David Naggar, one of Amazon's negotiators, testified, whenever Amazon "would make a concession on an important deal point," it would "come back to us from another publisher asking for the same thing or proposing similar language." J.A. 1491.

Once again, Apple closely monitored the negotiations with Amazon. The Publisher Defendants would inform Cue when they had completed agency agreements, and his team monitored price changes on the Kindle. When Penguin languished behind the others, Cue informed Jobs that Apple was "changing a bunch of Penguin titles to 9.99" in the iBookstore "because they didn't get their Amazon deal done." *Apple*, 952 F.Supp.2d at 682 (internal quotation marks omitted). By March 2010, Macmillan, HarperCollins, Hachette, and Simon & Schuster had completed agency agreements with Amazon. When Penguin completed its deal in June, the company's executive proudly announced to Cue that "[t]he playing field is now level." *Id.* (internal quotation marks omitted).[12]

F. EFFECT ON EBOOK PRICES

As Apple and the Publisher Defendants expected, the iBookstore price caps quickly became the benchmark for ebook versions of new releases and *New York Times* bestsellers. In the five months following the launch of the iBookstore, the publishers who joined the marketplace and switched Amazon to an agency model priced 85.7% of new releases on Kindle and 92.1% of new releases on the iBookstore at, or just below, the price caps. *Apple*, 952 F.Supp.2d at 682. Prices for *New York Times* bestsellers took a similar leap as publishers began to sell

96.8% of their bestsellers on Kindle and 99.4% of their bestsellers on the iBookstore at, or just below, the Apple price caps. *Id.* During that same time period, Random House, which had not switched to an agency model, saw virtually no change in the prices for its new releases or *New York Times* bestsellers.

The Apple price caps also had a ripple effect on the rest of the Publisher Defendants' catalogues. Recognizing that Apple's price caps were tied to the price of hardcover books, many of these publishers increased the prices of their newly released hardcover books to shift the ebook version into a higher price category. *Id.* at 683. Furthermore, because the Publisher Defendants who switched to the agency model expected to make less money per sale than under the wholesale model, they also increased the prices on their ebooks that were not new releases or bestsellers to make up for the expected loss of revenue.[13] Based on data from February 2010—just before the Publisher Defendants switched Amazon to agency pricing—to February 2011, an expert retained by the Justice Department observed that the weighted average price of the Publisher Defendants' new releases increased by 24.2%, while bestsellers increased by 40.4%, and other ebooks increased by 27.5%, for a total weighted average ebook price increase of 23.9%.14 Indeed, even Apple's expert agreed, noting that, over a two-year period, the Publisher Defendants increased their average prices for hardcovers, new releases, and other ebooks.

Increasing prices reduced demand for the Publisher Defendants' ebooks. According to one of Plaintiffs' experts, the publishers who switched to agency sold 77,307 fewer ebooks over a two-week period after the switch to agency than in a comparable two-week period before the switch, which amounted to selling 12.9% fewer units. *Id.* at 684. Another expert relied on data from Random House to estimate how many ebooks the Publisher Defendants who switched Amazon to agency would have sold had they stayed with the wholesale model, and concluded that the agency switch and price increases led to 14.5% fewer sales. *Id.*

Significantly, these changes took place against the backdrop of a rapidly changing ebook market. Amazon introduced the Kindle in November 2007, just over two years before Apple launched the iPad in January 2010. During that short period, Apple estimated that the market grew from $70 million in ebook sales in 2007 to $280 million in 2009, and the company projected those figures to grow significantly in following years. Apple's expert witnesses argued that overall ebook sales continued to grow in the two years after the creation of the iBookstore and that the average ebook price fell during those years. But as Plaintiffs' experts pointed out, the ebook market had been expanding rapidly even before Apple's entry and average prices had been falling as lower-end publishers entered the market and larger numbers of old books became available in digital form. "Apple's experts did not present any analysis that attempted to control for the many changes that the e-book market was experiencing during these early years of its growth," *Apple*, 952 F.Supp.2d at 685, nor did they estimate how the market would have grown but for Apple's agreement with the Publisher Defendants to switch to an agency model and raise prices. To the contrary, the undisputed fact that the Publisher Defendants raised prices on their ebooks, which accounted for roughly 50% of the trade ebook market in the first quarter of 2010, necessitated "a finding that the actions taken by

Apple and the Publisher Defendants led to an increase in the price of e-books." *Id.*

Finally, in response to the dissent's claim that Apple's conduct "deconcentrat[ed] ... the e-book retail market" and thus was "pro-competitive," Dissenting Op. at 31, it is worth noting that the district court's economic analysis and the parties' submissions at trial focused entirely on the price and sales figures for trade ebooks. This is because both parties agreed that the relevant market in this case is "the trade e-books market, not the e-reader market or the 'e-books system' market." *United States v. Apple, Inc.*, 889 F.Supp.2d 623, 642 (S.D.N.Y.2012); *Apple*, 952 F.Supp.2d at 694 n. 60. The district court did not analyze the state of competition between ebook retailers or determine that Amazon's pricing policy acted, as the dissent accuses, as a "barrier[ ] to entry" for other potential retailers. Dissenting Op. at 24, 30.

1. The judge writes in the verdict that Apple attempted to create an ebook monopoly by controlling price. As she notes, however, the dissenting opinions from the lower court suggest that what Apple did was not a monopolistic action, but a competitive act, because they were trying to compete with Amazon. Based on what you've learned so far and the facts laid out in this case, do you think Apple's behavior was legal?

EXCERPT FROM *US V. MICROSOFT CORPORATION*, BY COLLEEN KOLLAR-KOTELLY, UNITED STATES DISTRICT COURT FOR THE DISTRICT OF COLUMBIA, NOVEMBER 12, 2002

FINAL JUDGMENT

WHEREAS, plaintiffs United States of America ("United States") and the States of New York, Ohio, Illinois, Kentucky, Louisiana, Maryland, Michigan, North Carolina and Wisconsin and defendant Microsoft Corporation ("Microsoft"), by their respective attorneys, have consented to the entry of this Final Judgment;

AND WHEREAS, this Final Judgment does not constitute any admission by any party regarding any issue of fact or law;

AND WHEREAS, Microsoft agrees to be bound by the provisions of this Final Judgment pending its approval by the Court;

NOW THEREFORE, upon remand from the United States Court of Appeals for the District of Columbia Circuit, and upon the consent of the aforementioned parties, it is hereby ORDERED, ADJUDGED, AND DECREED:

I. JURISDICTION

This Court has jurisdiction of the subject matter of this action and of the person of Microsoft.

II. APPLICABILITY

This Final Judgment applies to Microsoft and to each of its officers, directors, agents, employees, subsidiaries, successors and assigns; and to all other persons in active concert or participation with any of them who shall have received actual notice of this Final Judgment by personal service or otherwise.

III. PROHIBITED CONDUCT

A. Microsoft shall not retaliate against an OEM by altering Microsoft's commercial relations with that OEM, or by withholding newly introduced forms of non-monetary Consideration (including but not limited to new versions of existing forms of non-monetary Consideration) from that OEM, because it is known to Microsoft that the OEM is or is contemplating:

1. developing, distributing, promoting, using, selling, or licensing any software that competes with Microsoft Platform Software or any product or service that distributes or promotes any Non-Microsoft Middleware;

2. shipping a Personal Computer that (a) includes both a Windows Operating System Product and a non-Microsoft Operating System, or (b) will boot with more than one Operating System; or

3. exercising any of the options or alternatives provided for under this Final Judgment.

Nothing in this provision shall prohibit Microsoft from enforcing any provision of any license with any OEM or any intellectual property right that is not inconsistent with this Final Judgment. Microsoft shall not terminate a Covered OEM's license for a Windows Operating System Product without having first given the Covered OEM written notice of the reasons for the proposed termination and not less than thirty days' opportunity to cure. Notwithstanding the foregoing, Microsoft shall have no obligation to provide such a termination notice and opportunity to cure to any Covered OEM that has received two or more such notices during the term of its Windows Operating System Product license.

Nothing in this provision shall prohibit Microsoft from providing Consideration to any OEM with respect to any Microsoft product or service where that Consideration is commensurate with the absolute level or amount of that OEM's development, distribution, promotion, or licensing of that Microsoft product or service.

B. Microsoft's provision of Windows Operating System Products to Covered OEMs shall be pursuant to uniform license agreements with uniform terms and conditions. Without limiting the foregoing, Microsoft shall charge each Covered OEM the applicable royalty for Windows Operating System Products as set forth on a schedule, to be established by Microsoft and published on a web site accessible to the Plaintiffs and all Covered OEMs, that provides for uniform royalties for Windows Operating System Products, except that:

1. the schedule may specify different royalties for different language versions;

2. the schedule may specify reasonable volume discounts based upon the actual volume of licenses of any Windows Operating System Product or any group of such products; and

3. the schedule may include market development allowances, programs, or other discounts in connection with Windows Operating System Products, provided that:

   a. such discounts are offered and available uniformly to all Covered OEMs, except that Microsoft may establish one uniform discount schedule for the ten largest Covered OEMs and a second uniform discount schedule for the eleventh through twentieth largest Covered OEMs, where the size of the OEM is measured by volume of licenses;

   b. such discounts are based on objective, verifiable criteria that shall be applied and enforced on a uniform basis for all Covered OEMs; and

   c. such discounts or their award shall not be based on or impose any criterion or requirement that is otherwise inconsistent with any portion of this Final Judgment.

C. Microsoft shall not restrict by agreement any OEM licensee from exercising any of the following options or alternatives:

1. Installing, and displaying icons, shortcuts, or menu entries for, any Non-Microsoft Middleware or any product or service (including but not limited to IAP products or services) that distributes, uses, promotes, or supports any Non-Microsoft Middleware, on the desktop or Start menu, or anywhere else in a Windows Operating System Product where a list of icons, shortcuts, or menu entries for applications are generally displayed, except that Microsoft may restrict an OEM from displaying icons, shortcuts and menu entries for any product in any list of such icons, shortcuts, or menu entries specified in the Windows documentation as being limited to products that provide particular types of functionality, provided that the restrictions are non-discriminatory with respect to non-Microsoft and Microsoft products.

2. Distributing or promoting Non-Microsoft Middleware by installing and displaying on the desktop shortcuts of any size or shape so long as such shortcuts do not impair the functionality of the user interface.

3. Launching automatically, at the conclusion of the initial boot sequence or subsequent boot sequences, or upon connections to or disconnections from the Internet, any Non-Microsoft Middleware if a Microsoft Middleware Product that provides similar functionality would otherwise be launched automatically at that time, provided that any such Non-Microsoft Middleware displays on the desktop no user interface or a user interface of similar size and shape to the user interface displayed by the corresponding Microsoft Middleware Product.

4. Offering users the option of launching other Operating Systems from the Basic Input/Output System or a non-Microsoft boot-loader or similar program that launches prior to the start of the Windows Operating System Product.

5. Presenting in the initial boot sequence its own IAP offer provided that the OEM complies with reasonable technical specifications established by Microsoft, including a requirement that the end user be returned to the initial boot sequence upon the conclusion of any such offer.

6. Exercising any of the options provided in Section III.H of this Final Judgment.

D. Starting at the earlier of the release of Service Pack 1 for Windows XP or 12 months after the submission of this Final Judgment to the Court, Microsoft shall disclose to ISVs, IHVs, IAPs, ICPs, and OEMs, for the sole purpose of interoperating with a Windows Operating System Product, via the Microsoft Developer Network ("MSDN") or similar mechanisms, the APIs and related Documentation that are used by Microsoft Middleware to interoperate with a Windows Operating System Product. For purposes of this Section III.D, the term APIs means the interfaces, including any associated callback interfaces, that Microsoft Middleware running on a Windows Operating System Product uses to call upon that Windows Operating System Product in order to obtain any services from that Windows Operating System Product. In the case of a new major version of Microsoft Middleware, the disclosures required by this Section III.D shall occur no later than the last major beta test release of that Microsoft Middleware. In the case of a new version of a Windows Operating System Product, the obligations imposed by this Section III.D shall occur in a Timely Manner.

E. Starting nine months after the submission of this proposed Final Judgment to the Court, Microsoft shall make available for use by third parties, for the sole purpose of interoperating or communicating with a Windows Operating System Product, on reasonable and non-discriminatory terms (consistent with Section III.I), any Communications Protocol that is, on or after the date this Final Judgment is submitted to the Court, (i) implemented in a Windows Operating System Product installed on a client computer, and (ii) used to interoperate, or communicate, natively (i.e., without the addition of software code to the client operating system product) with a Microsoft server operating system product.

F.

1. Microsoft shall not retaliate against any ISV or IHV because of that ISV's or IHV's:

   a. developing, using, distributing, promoting or supporting any software that competes with Microsoft Platform Software or any software that runs on any software that competes with Microsoft Platform Software, or

   b. exercising any of the options or alternatives provided for under this Final Judgment.

2. Microsoft shall not enter into any agreement relating to a Windows Operating System Product that conditions the grant of any Consideration on an ISV's refraining from developing, using, distributing, or promoting any software that competes with Microsoft Platform Software or any software that runs on any software that competes with Microsoft Platform Software, except that Microsoft may enter into agreements that place limitations on an ISV's development, use, distribution or promotion of any such software if those limitations are reasonably necessary to and of reasonable scope and duration in relation to a bona fide contractual obligation of the ISV to use, distribute or promote any Microsoft software or to develop software for, or in conjunction with, Microsoft.

3. Nothing in this section shall prohibit Microsoft from enforcing any provision of any agreement with any ISV or IHV, or any intellectual property right, that is not inconsistent with this Final Judgment.

G. Microsoft shall not enter into any agreement with:

1. any IAP, ICP, ISV, IHV or OEM that grants Consideration on the condition that such entity distributes, promotes, uses, or supports, exclusively or in a fixed percentage, any Microsoft Platform Software, except that Microsoft may enter into agreements in which such an entity agrees to distribute, promote, use or support Microsoft Platform Software in a fixed percentage whenever Microsoft in good faith obtains a representation that it is commercially practicable for the entity to provide equal or greater

distribution, promotion, use or support for software that competes with Microsoft Platform Software, or

2. any IAP or ICP that grants placement on the desktop or elsewhere in any Windows Operating System Product to that IAP or ICP on the condition that the IAP or ICP refrain from distributing, promoting or using any software that competes with Microsoft Middleware.

Nothing in this section shall prohibit Microsoft from entering into (a) any bona fide joint venture or (b) any joint development or joint services arrangement with any ISV, IHV, IAP, ICP, or OEM for a new product, technology or service, or any material value-add to an existing product, technology or service, in which both Microsoft and the ISV, IHV, IAP, ICP, or OEM contribute significant developer or other resources, that prohibits such entity from competing with the object of the joint venture or other arrangement for a reasonable period of time.

This Section does not apply to any agreements in which Microsoft licenses intellectual property in from a third party.

H. Starting at the earlier of the release of Service Pack 1 for Windows XP or 12 months after the submission of this Final Judgment to the Court, Microsoft shall:

1. Allow end users (via a mechanism readily accessible from the desktop or Start menu such as an Add/Remove icon) and OEMs (via standard preinstallation kits) to enable or remove access to each Microsoft

Middleware Product or Non-Microsoft Middleware Product by (a) displaying or removing icons, shortcuts, or menu entries on the desktop or Start menu, or anywhere else in a Windows Operating System Product where a list of icons, shortcuts, or menu entries for applications are generally displayed, except that Microsoft may restrict the display of icons, shortcuts, or menu entries for any product in any list of such icons, shortcuts, or menu entries specified in the Windows documentation as being limited to products that provide particular types of functionality, provided that the restrictions are non-discriminatory with respect to non-Microsoft and Microsoft products; and (b) enabling or disabling automatic invocations pursuant to Section III.C.3 of this Final Judgment that are used to launch Non-Microsoft Middleware Products or Microsoft Middleware Products. The mechanism shall offer the end user a separate and unbiased choice with respect to enabling or removing access (as described in this subsection III.H.1) and altering default invocations (as described in the following subsection III.H.2) with regard to each such Microsoft Middleware Product or Non-Microsoft Middleware Product and may offer the end-user a separate and unbiased choice of enabling or removing access and altering default configurations as to all Microsoft Middleware Products as a group or all Non-Microsoft Middleware Products as a group.

2. Allow end users (via an unbiased mechanism readily available from the desktop or Start menu), OEMs (via standard OEM preinstallation kits), and Non-Microsoft Middleware Products (via a mechanism

which may, at Microsoft's option, require confirmation from the end user in an unbiased manner) to designate a Non-Microsoft Middleware Product to be invoked in place of that Microsoft Middleware Product (or vice versa) in any case where the Windows Operating System Product would otherwise launch the Microsoft Middleware Product in a separate Top-Level Window and display either (i) all of the user interface elements or (ii) the Trademark of the Microsoft Middleware Product.

Notwithstanding the foregoing Section III.H.2, the Windows Operating System Product may invoke a Microsoft Middleware Product in any instance in which:

a. that Microsoft Middleware Product would be invoked solely for use in interoperating with a server maintained by Microsoft (outside the context of general Web browsing), or

b. that designated Non-Microsoft Middleware Product fails to implement a reasonable technical requirement (e.g., a requirement to be able to host a particular ActiveX control) that is necessary for valid technical reasons to supply the end user with functionality consistent with a Windows Operating System Product, provided that the technical reasons are described in a reasonably prompt manner to any ISV that requests them.

3. Ensure that a Windows Operating System Product does not (a) automatically alter an OEM's configuration of icons, shortcuts or menu entries installed

or displayed by the OEM pursuant to Section III.C of this Final Judgment without first seeking confirmation from the user and (b) seek such confirmation from the end user for an automatic (as opposed to user-initiated) alteration of the OEM's configuration until 14 days after the initial boot up of a new Personal Computer. Any such automatic alteration and confirmation shall be unbiased with respect to Microsoft Middleware Products and Non-Microsoft Middleware. Microsoft shall not alter the manner in which a Windows Operating System Product automatically alters an OEM's configuration of icons, shortcuts or menu entries other than in a new version of a Windows Operating System Product.

Microsoft's obligations under this Section III.H as to any new Windows Operating System Product shall be determined based on the Microsoft Middleware Products which exist seven months prior to the last beta test version (i.e., the one immediately preceding the first release candidate) of that Windows Operating System Product.

I. Microsoft shall offer to license to ISVs, IHVs, IAPs, ICPs, and OEMs any intellectual property rights owned or licensable by Microsoft that are required to exercise any of the options or alternatives expressly provided to them under this Final Judgment, provided that

1. all terms, including royalties or other payment of monetary consideration, are reasonable and non-discriminatory;

2. the scope of any such license (and the intellectual property rights licensed thereunder) need be no broader than is necessary to ensure that an ISV, IHV, IAP, ICP or OEM is able to exercise the options or alternatives expressly provided under this Final Judgment (e.g., an ISV's, IHV's, IAP's, ICP's and OEM's option to promote Non-Microsoft Middleware shall not confer any rights to any Microsoft intellectual property rights infringed by that Non-Microsoft Middleware);

3. an ISV's, IHV's, IAP's, ICP's, or OEM's rights may be conditioned on its not assigning, transferring or sub-licensing its rights under any license granted under this provision; and

4. the terms of any license granted under this section are in all respects consistent with the express terms of this Final Judgment.

Beyond the express terms of any license granted by Microsoft pursuant to this section, this Final Judgment does not, directly or by implication, estoppel or otherwise, confer any rights, licenses, covenants or immunities with regard to any Microsoft intellectual property to anyone.

J. No provision of this Final Judgment shall:

1. Require Microsoft to document, disclose or license to third parties: (a) portions of APIs or Documentation or portions or layers of Communications Protocols the disclosure of which would compromise the security of a particular installation or group of instal-

lations of anti-piracy, anti-virus, software licensing, digital rights management, encryption or authentication systems, including without limitation, keys, authorization tokens or enforcement criteria; or (b) any API, interface or other information related to any Microsoft product if lawfully directed not to do so by a governmental agency of competent jurisdiction.

2. Prevent Microsoft from conditioning any license of any API, Documentation or Communications Protocol related to anti-piracy systems, anti-virus technologies, license enforcement mechanisms, authentication/authorization security, or third party intellectual property protection mechanisms of any Microsoft product to any person or entity on the requirement that the licensee: (a) has no history of software counterfeiting or piracy or willful violation of intellectual property rights, (b) has a reasonable business need for the API, Documentation or Communications Protocol for a planned or shipping product, (c) meets reasonable, objective standards established by Microsoft for certifying the authenticity and viability of its business, (d) agrees to submit, at its own expense, any computer program using such APIs, Documentation or Communication Protocols to third-party verification, approved by Microsoft, to test for and ensure verification and compliance with Microsoft specifications for use of the API or interface, which specifications shall be related to

proper operation and integrity of the systems and mechanisms identified in this paragraph.

IV. COMPLIANCE AND ENFORCEMENT PROCEDURES

A. ENFORCEMENT AUTHORITY

1. The Plaintiffs shall have exclusive responsibility for enforcing this Final Judgment. Without in any way limiting the sovereign enforcement authority of each of the plaintiff States, the plaintiff States shall form a committee to coordinate their enforcement of this Final Judgment. A plaintiff State shall take no action to enforce this Final Judgment without first consulting with the United States and with the plaintiff States' enforcement committee.

2. To determine and enforce compliance with this Final Judgment, duly authorized representatives of the United States and the plaintiff States, on reasonable notice to Microsoft and subject to any lawful privilege, shall be permitted the following:

   a. Access during normal office hours to inspect any and all source code, books, ledgers, accounts, correspondence, memoranda and other documents and records in the possession, custody, or control of Microsoft, which may have counsel present, regarding any matters contained in this Final Judgment.

b. Subject to the reasonable convenience of Microsoft and without restraint or interference from it, to interview, informally or on the record, officers, employees, or agents of Microsoft, who may have counsel present, regarding any matters contained in this Final Judgment.

c. Upon written request of the United States or a duly designated representative of a plaintiff State, on reasonable notice given to Microsoft, Microsoft shall submit such written reports under oath as requested regarding any matters contained in this Final Judgment.

Individual plaintiff States will consult with the plaintiff States' enforcement committee to minimize the duplication and burden of the exercise of the foregoing powers, where practicable.

1. The Plaintiffs shall not disclose any information or documents obtained from Microsoft under this Final Judgment except for the purpose of securing compliance with this Final Judgment, in a legal proceeding to which one or more of the Plaintiffs is a party, or as otherwise required by law; provided that the relevant Plaintiff(s) must provide ten days' advance notice to Microsoft before disclosing in any legal proceeding (other than a grand jury proceed-

ing) to which Microsoft is not a party any information or documents provided by Microsoft pursuant to this Final Judgment which Microsoft has identified in writing as material as to which a claim of protection may be asserted under Rule 26(c)(7) of the Federal Rules of Civil Procedure.

2. The Plaintiffs shall have the authority to seek such orders as are necessary from the Court to enforce this Final Judgment, provided, however, that the Plaintiffs shall afford Microsoft a reasonable opportunity to cure alleged violations of Sections III.C, III.D, III.E and III.H, provided further that any action by Microsoft to cure any such violation shall not be a defense to enforcement with respect to any knowing, willful or systematic violations.

B. APPOINTMENT OF A TECHNICAL COMMITTEE

1. Within 30 days of entry of this Final Judgment, the parties shall create and recommend to the Court for its appointment a three-person Technical Committee ("TC") to assist in enforcement of and compliance with this Final Judgment.

2. The TC members shall be experts in software design and programming. No TC member shall have a conflict of interest that could prevent him or her from performing his or her duties under this Final Judgment in a fair and unbiased manner. Without limitation to the foregoing, no TC member (absent the agreement of both parties):

a. shall have been employed in any capacity by Microsoft or any competitor to Microsoft within the past year, nor shall she or he be so employed during his or her term on the TC;

b. shall have been retained as a consulting or testifying expert by any person in this action or in any other action adverse to or on behalf of Microsoft; or

c. shall perform any other work for Microsoft or any competitor of Microsoft for two years after the expiration of the term of his or her service on the TC.

1. Within 7 days of entry of this Final Judgment, the Plaintiffs as a group and Microsoft shall each select one member of the TC, and those two members shall then select the third member. The selection and approval process shall proceed as follows.

a. As soon as practicable after submission of this Final Judgment to the Court, the Plaintiffs as a group and Microsoft shall each identify to the other the individual it proposes to select as its designee to the TC. The Plaintiffs and Microsoft shall not object to each other's selection on any ground other than failure to satisfy the requirements of Section IV.B.2 above. Any such objection shall be made within ten business days of the receipt of notification of selection.

b. The Plaintiffs shall apply to the Court for appointment of the persons selected by the Plaintiffs and Microsoft pursuant to Section

IV.B.3.a above. Any objections to the eligibility of a selected person that the parties have failed to resolve between themselves shall be decided by the Court based solely on the requirements stated in Section IV.B.2 above.

c. As soon as practical after their appointment by the Court, the two members of the TC selected by the Plaintiffs and Microsoft (the "Standing Committee Members") shall identify to the Plaintiffs and Microsoft the person that they in turn propose to select as the third member of the TC. The Plaintiffs and Microsoft shall not object to this selection on any grounds other than failure to satisfy the requirements of Section IV.B.2 above. Any such objection shall be made within ten business days of the receipt of notification of the selection and shall be served on the other party as well as on the Standing Committee Members.

d. The Plaintiffs shall apply to the Court for appointment of the person selected by the Standing Committee Members. If the Standing Committee Members cannot agree on a third member of the TC, the third member shall be appointed by the Court. Any objection by Microsoft or the Plaintiffs to the eligibility of the person selected by the Standing Committee Members which the parties have failed to resolve among themselves shall also be decided by the Court based on the requirements stated in Section IV.B.2 above.

1. Each TC member shall serve for an initial term of 30 months. At the end of a TC member's initial 30-month term, the party that originally selected him or her may, in its sole discretion, either request re-appointment by the Court to a second 30-month term or replace the TC member in the same manner as provided for in Section IV.B.3.a above. In the case of the third member of the TC, that member shall be re-appointed or replaced in the manner provided in Section IV.B.3.c above.

2. If the United States determines that a member of the TC has failed to act diligently and consistently with the purposes of this Final Judgment, or if a member of the TC resigns, or for any other reason ceases to serve in his or her capacity as a member of the TC, the person or persons that originally selected the TC member shall select a replacement member in the same manner as provided for in Section IV.B.3.

3. Promptly after appointment of the TC by the Court, the United States shall enter into a Technical Committee services agreement ("TC Services Agreement") with each TC member that grants the rights, powers and authorities necessary to permit the TC to perform its duties under this Final Judgment. Microsoft shall indemnify each TC member and hold him or her harmless against any losses, claims, damages, liabilities or expenses arising out of, or in connection with, the performance of the TC's duties, except to the extent that such liabilities, losses, damages, claims, or expenses result from misfeasance, gross negligence, willful or wanton acts, or bad faith by the TC member. The TC Services Agreements shall include the following.

a. The TC members shall serve, without bond or other security, at the cost and expense of Microsoft on such terms and conditions as the Plaintiffs approve, including the payment of reasonable fees and expenses.

b. The TC Services Agreement shall provide that each member of the TC shall comply with the limitations provided for in Section IV.B.2 above.

1. Microsoft shall provide the TC with a permanent office, telephone, and other office support facilities at Microsoft's corporate campus in Redmond, Washington. Microsoft shall also, upon reasonable advance notice from the TC, provide the TC with reasonable access to available office space, telephone, and other office support facilities at any other Microsoft facility identified by the TC.

2. The TC shall have the following powers and duties:

a. The TC shall have the power and authority to monitor Microsoft's compliance with its obligations under this final judgment.

b. The TC may, on reasonable notice to Microsoft:

i. interview, either informally or on the record, any Microsoft personnel, who may have counsel present; any such interview to be subject to the reasonable convenience of such personnel and without restraint or interference by Microsoft;

ii. inspect and copy any document in the

possession, custody or control of Microsoft personnel;

iii. obtain reasonable access to any systems or equipment to which Microsoft personnel have access;

iv. obtain access to, and inspect, any physical facility, building or other premises to which Microsoft personnel have access; and

v. require Microsoft personnel to provide compilations of documents, data and other information, and to submit reports to the TC containing such material, in such form as the TC may reasonably direct.

a. The TC shall have access to Microsoft's source code, subject to the terms of Microsoft's standard source code Confidentiality Agreement, as approved by the Plaintiffs and to be agreed to by the TC members pursuant to Section IV.B.9 below, and by any staff or consultants who may have access to the source code. The TC may study, interrogate and interact with the source code in order to perform its functions and duties, including the handling of complaints and other inquiries from non-parties.

b. The TC shall receive complaints from the Compliance Officer, third parties or the Plaintiffs and handle them in the manner specified in Section IV.D below.

c. The TC shall report in writing to the Plaintiffs every six months until expiration of this Final Judgment the actions it has undertaken in performing its duties pursuant to this Final Judgment, including the identification of each business practice reviewed and any recommendations made by the TC.

d. Regardless of when reports are due, when the TC has reason to believe that there may have been a failure by Microsoft to comply with any term of this Final Judgment, the TC shall immediately notify the Plaintiffs in writing setting forth the relevant details.

e. TC members may communicate with non-parties about how their complaints or inquiries might be resolved with Microsoft, so long as the confidentiality of information obtained from Microsoft is maintained.

f. The TC may hire at the cost and expense of Microsoft, with prior notice to Microsoft and subject to approval by the Plaintiffs, such staff or consultants (all of whom must meet the qualifications of Section IV.B.2) as are reasonably necessary for the TC to carry out its duties and responsibilities under this Final Judgment. The compensation of any person retained by the TC shall be based on reasonable and customary terms commensurate with the individual's experience and responsibilities.

g. The TC shall account for all reasonable expenses incurred, including agreed upon fees for the TC members' services, subject to the approval of the Plaintiffs. Microsoft may, on application to the Court, object to the reasonableness of any such fees or other expenses. On any such application: (a) the burden shall be on Microsoft to demonstrate unreasonableness; and (b) the TC member(s) shall be entitled to recover all costs incurred on such application (including reasonable attorneys' fees and costs), regardless of the Court's disposition of such application, unless the Court shall expressly find that the TC's opposition to the application was without substantial justification.

1. Each TC member, and any consultants or staff hired by the TC, shall sign a confidentiality agreement prohibiting disclosure of any information obtained in the course of performing his or her duties as a member of the TC or as a person assisting the TC to anyone other than Microsoft, the Plaintiffs, or the Court. All information gathered by the TC in connection with this Final Judgment and any report and recommendations prepared by the TC shall be treated as Highly Confidential under the Protective Order in this case, and shall not be disclosed to any person other than Microsoft and the Plaintiffs except as allowed by the Protective Order entered in the Action or by further order of this Court.

2. No member of the TC shall make any public statements relating to the TC's activities.

C. APPOINTMENT OF A MICROSOFT INTERNAL COMPLIANCE OFFICER

1. Microsoft shall designate, within 30 days of entry of this Final Judgment, an internal Compliance Officer who shall be an employee of Microsoft with responsibility for administering Microsoft's antitrust compliance program and helping to ensure compliance with this Final Judgment.

2. The Compliance Officer shall supervise the review of Microsoft's activities to ensure that they comply with this Final Judgment. He or she may be assisted by other employees of Microsoft.

3. The Compliance Officer shall be responsible for performing the following activities:

   a. within 30 days after entry of this Final Judgment, distributing a copy of the Final Judgment to all officers and directors of Microsoft;

   b. promptly distributing a copy of this Final Judgment to any person who succeeds to a position described in Section IV.C.3.a above;

   c. ensuring that those persons designated in Section IV.C.3.a above are annually briefed on the meaning and requirements of this Final Judgment and the U.S. antitrust laws and advising them that Microsoft's legal advisors are available to confer with them regarding any question concerning compliance with this Final Judgment or under the U.S. antitrust laws;

d. obtaining from each person designated in Section IV.C.3.a above an annual written certification that he or she: (i) has read and agrees to abide by the terms of this Final Judgment; and (ii) has been advised and understands that his or her failure to comply with this Final Judgment may result in a finding of contempt of court;

e. maintaining a record of all persons to whom a copy of this Final Judgment has been distributed and from whom the certification described in Section IV.C.3.d above has been obtained;

f. establishing and maintaining the website provided for in Section IV.D.3.b below.

g. receiving complaints from third parties, the TC and the Plaintiffs concerning Microsoft's compliance with this Final Judgment and following the appropriate procedures set forth in Section IV.D below; and

    h. maintaining a record of all complaints received and action taken by Microsoft with respect to each such complaint.

D. VOLUNTARY DISPUTE RESOLUTION

1. Third parties may submit complaints concerning Microsoft's compliance with this Final Judgment to the Plaintiffs, the TC or the Compliance Officer.

2. In order to enhance the ability of the Plaintiffs to enforce compliance with this Final Judgment, and to advance the parties' joint interest and the public interest in prompt resolution of issues and disputes, the parties have agreed that the TC and the Compliance Officer shall have the following additional responsibilities.

3. Submissions to the Compliance Officer.

    a. Third parties, the TC, or the Plaintiffs in their discretion may submit to the Compliance Officer any complaints concerning Microsoft's compliance with this Final Judgment. Without in any way limiting its authority to take any other action to enforce this Final Judgment, the Plaintiffs may submit complaints related to Sections III.C, III.D, III.E and III.H to the Compliance Officer whenever doing so would be consistent with the public interest.

b. To facilitate the communication of complaints and inquiries by third parties, the Compliance Officer shall place on Microsoft's Internet website, in a manner acceptable to the Plaintiffs, the procedures for submitting complaints. To encourage whenever possible the informal resolution of complaints and inquiries, the website shall provide a mechanism for communicating complaints and inquiries to the Compliance Officer.

c. Microsoft shall have 30 days after receiving a complaint to attempt to resolve it or reject it, and will then promptly advise the TC of the nature of the complaint and its disposition.

d. Submissions to the TC.

e. The Compliance Officer, third parties or the Plaintiffs in their discretion may submit to the TC any complaints concerning Microsoft's compliance with this Final Judgment.

f. The TC shall investigate complaints received and will consult with the Plaintiffs regarding its investigation. At least once during its investigation, and more often when it may help resolve complaints informally, the TC shall meet with the Compliance Officer to allow Microsoft to respond to the substance of the complaint and to determine whether the complaint can be resolved without further proceedings.

g. If the TC concludes that a complaint is meritorious, it shall advise Microsoft and the Plaintiffs of its conclusion and its proposal for cure.

h. No work product, findings or recommendations by the TC may be admitted in any enforcement proceeding before the Court for any purpose, and no member of the TC shall testify by deposition, in court or before any other tribunal regarding any matter related to this Final Judgment.

i. The TC may preserve the anonymity of any third party complainant where it deems it appropriate to do so upon the request of the Plaintiffs or the third party, or in its discretion.

V. TERMINATION

a. Unless this Court grants an extension, this Final Judgment will expire on the fifth anniversary of the date it is entered by the Court.

b. In any enforcement proceeding in which the Court has found that Microsoft has engaged in a pattern of willful and systematic violations, the Plaintiffs may apply to the Court for a one-time extension of this Final Judgment of up to two years, together with such other relief as the Court may deem appropriate.

VI. DEFINITIONS

a. "API" means application programming interface, including any interface that Microsoft is obligated to disclose pursuant to III.D.

b. "Communications Protocol" means the set of rules for information exchange to accomplish predefined tasks between a Windows Operating System Product and a server operating system product connected via a network, including, but not limited to, a local area network, a wide area network or the Internet. These rules govern the format, semantics, timing, sequencing, and error control of messages exchanged over a network.

c. "Consideration" means any monetary payment or the provision of preferential licensing terms; technical, marketing, and sales support; enabling programs; product information; information about future plans; developer support; hardware or software certification or approval; or permission to display trademarks, icons or logos.

d. "Covered OEMs" means the 20 OEMs with the highest worldwide volume of licenses of Windows Operating System Products reported to Microsoft in Microsoft's fiscal year preceding the effective date of the Final Judgment. The OEMs that fall within this definition of Covered OEMs shall be recomputed by Microsoft as soon as practicable after the close of each of Microsoft's fiscal years.

e. "Documentation" means all information regarding the identification and means of using APIs that a person of ordinary skill in the art requires to make effective use of those APIs. Such information shall be of the sort and to the level of specificity, precision and detail that Microsoft customarily provides for APIs it documents in the Microsoft Developer Network ("MSDN").

f. "IAP" means an Internet access provider that provides consumers with a connection to the Internet, with or without its own proprietary content.

g. "ICP" means an Internet content provider that provides content to users of the Internet by maintaining Web sites.

h. "IHV" means an independent hardware vendor that develops hardware to be included in or used with a Personal Computer running a Windows Operating System Product.

i. "ISV" means an entity other than Microsoft that is engaged in the development or marketing of software products.

j. "Microsoft Middleware" means software code that

1. Microsoft distributes separately from a Windows Operating System Product to update that Windows Operating System Product;

2. is Trademarked or is marketed by Microsoft as a major version of any Microsoft Middleware Product defined in section VI.K.1; and

3. provides the same or substantially similar functionality as a Microsoft Middleware Product.

Microsoft Middleware shall include at least the software code that controls most or all of the user interface elements of that Microsoft Middleware.

Software code described as part of, and distributed separately to update, a Microsoft Middleware Product shall not be deemed Microsoft Middleware unless identified as a new major version of that Microsoft Middleware Product. A major version shall be identified by a whole number or by a number with just a single digit to the right of the decimal point.

a. "Microsoft Middleware Product" means

1. the functionality provided by Internet Explorer, Microsoft's Java Virtual Machine, Windows Media Player, Windows Messenger, Outlook Express and their successors in a Windows Operating System Product, and

2. for any functionality that is first licensed, distributed or sold by Microsoft after the entry of this Final Judgment and that is part of any Windows Operating System Product

i. Internet browsers, email client software, networked audio/video client software, instant messaging software or

ii. functionality provided by Microsoft software that --

iii. is, or in the year preceding the commercial release of any new Windows Operating System Product was, distributed separately by Microsoft (or by an entity acquired by Microsoft) from a Windows Operating System Product;

iv. is similar to the functionality provided by a Non-Microsoft Middleware Product; and

v. is Trademarked.

Functionality that Microsoft describes or markets as being part of a Microsoft Middleware Product (such as a service pack, upgrade, or bug fix for Internet Explorer), or that is a version of a Microsoft Middleware Product (such as Internet Explorer 5.5), shall be considered to be part of that Microsoft Middleware Product.

a. "Microsoft Platform Software" means (i) a Windows Operating System Product and/or (ii) a Microsoft Middleware Product.

b. "Non-Microsoft Middleware" means a non-Microsoft software product running on a Windows Operating System Product that exposes a range of functionality to ISVs through published APIs, and that could, if ported to or made interoperable with, a non-Microsoft Operating System, thereby make it easier for applications that rely in whole or in part on the functionality supplied by that software product to be ported to or run on that non-Microsoft Operating System.

c. "Non-Microsoft Middleware Product" means a non-Microsoft software product running on a Windows Operating System Product (i) that exposes a range of functionality to ISVs through published APIs, and that could, if ported to or made interoperable with, a non-Microsoft Operating System, thereby make it easier for applications that rely in whole or in part on the functionality supplied by that software product to be ported to or run on that non-Microsoft Operating System, and (ii) of which at least one million copies were distributed in the United States within the previous year.

d. "OEM" means an original equipment manufacturer of Personal Computers that is a licensee of a Windows Operating System Product.

e. "Operating System" means the software code that, inter alia, (i) controls the allocation and usage of hardware resources (such as the microprocessor and various peripheral devices) of a Personal Computer, (ii) provides a platform for developing applications by exposing functionality to ISVs through APIs, and (iii) supplies a user interface that enables users to access functionality of the operating system and in which they can run applications.

f. "Personal Computer" means any computer configured so that its primary purpose is for use by one person at a time, that uses a video display and keyboard (whether or not that video display and keyboard is included) and that contains an Intel x86 compatible (or successor) microprocessor. Servers, television set top boxes, handheld computers, game consoles, telephones, pagers, and personal digital assistants are examples of products that are not Personal Computers within the meaning of this definition.

g. "Timely Manner" means at the time Microsoft first releases a beta test version of a Windows Operating System Product that is made available via an MSDN subscription offering or of which 150,000 or more beta copies are distributed.

h. "Top-Level Window" means a window displayed by a Windows Operating System Product that (a) has its own window controls, such as move, resize, close, minimize, and maximize, (b) can contain sub-windows, and (c) contains user interface elements under the control of at least one independent process.

i. "Trademarked" means distributed in commerce and identified as distributed by a name other than Microsoft® or Windows® that Microsoft has claimed as a trademark or service mark by (i) marking the name with trademark notices, such as ® or TM, in connection with a product distributed in the United States; (ii) filing an application for trademark protection for the name in the United States Patent and Trademark Office; or (iii) asserting the name as a trademark in the United States in a demand letter or lawsuit. Any product distributed under descriptive or generic terms or a name comprised of the Microsoft® or Windows® trademarks together with descriptive or generic terms shall not be Trademarked as that term is used in this Final Judgment. Microsoft hereby disclaims any trademark rights in such descriptive or generic terms apart from the Microsoft® or Windows® trademarks, and hereby abandons any such rights that it may acquire in the future.

j. "Windows Operating System Product" means the software code (as opposed to source code) distributed commercially by Microsoft for use with Personal Computers as Windows 2000 Professional, Windows XP Home, Windows XP Professional, and successors to the foregoing, including the Personal Computer versions of the products currently code named "Longhorn" and "Blackcomb" and their successors, including upgrades, bug fixes, service packs, etc. The software code that comprises a Windows Operating System Product shall be determined by Microsoft in its sole discretion.

VII. FURTHER ELEMENTS

Jurisdiction is retained by this Court over this action such that the Court may act sua sponte to issue further orders or directions, including but not limited to orders or directions relating to the construction or carrying out of this Final Judgment, the enforcement of compliance therewith, the modification thereof, and the punishment of any violation thereof.

Jurisdiction is retained by this Court over this action and the parties thereto for the purpose of enabling either of the parties thereto to apply to this Court at any time for further orders and directions as may be necessary or appropriate to carry out or construe this Final Judgement, to modify or terminate any of its provisions, to enforce compliance, and to punish violations of its provisions.

VIII. THIRD PARTY RIGHTS

Nothing in this Final Judgement is intended to confer upon any other persons any rights or remedies of any nature whatsoever hereunder or by reason of this Final Judgement. SO ORDERED.

1. In overturning the lower court's verdict, Judge Kollar-Kotelly suggested that digital and tech companies should be held to a different standard when it comes to antitrust judgment. Do you agree with the judge's opinion?

2. The judgment prohibits Microsoft from interfering with users' abilities to use other non-Microsoft software or blocking that software from being used in place of Microsoft's own software. Why is this an important judgment in an antitrust case?

CHAPTER 4

WHAT ADVOCACY ORGANIZATIONS SAY

From start-up tech companies to digital media outlets to consumers' rights groups, the majority of the population is against digital trusts. People want choices when it comes to their technology, and they want to know how their digital landscape is being altered by the businesses that operate primarily in the digital world. To protect consumers and other businesses, advocates have promoted everything from net neutrality to digital antitrust legislation to keep these new monopolistic businesses in line. As you read this chapter you'll be asked to think about not only the businesses accused of being monopolies, but the parties that are hurt by that behavior.

"DIGITAL GRAB: CORPORATE POWER HAS SEIZED THE INTERNET," BY NORMAN SOLOMON, FROM *COMMON DREAMS*, MARCH 28, 2013

If your daily routine took you from one homegrown organic garden to another, bypassing vast fields choked with pesticides, you might feel pretty good about the current state of agriculture.

If your daily routine takes you from one noncommercial progressive website to another, you might feel pretty good about the current state of the Internet.

But while mass media have supplied endless raptures about a digital revolution, corporate power has seized the Internet -- and the anti-democratic grip is tightening every day.

"Most assessments of the Internet fail to ground it in political economy; they fail to understand the importance of capitalism in shaping and, for lack of a better term, domesticating the Internet," says Robert W. McChesney in his illuminating new book, *Digital Disconnect: How Capitalism is Turning the Internet Against Democracy.*

Plenty of commentators loudly celebrate the Internet. Some are vocal skeptics. "Both camps, with a few exceptions, have a single, deep, and often fatal flaw that severely compromises the value of their work," McChesney writes. "That flaw, simply put, is ignorance about really existing capitalism and an underappreciation of how capitalism dominates social life. . . . Both camps miss the way capitalism defines our times and sets the terms for understanding not only the Internet, but most everything else of a social nature, including politics, in our society."

159

And he adds: "The profit motive, commercialism, public relations, marketing, and advertising -- all defining features of contemporary corporate capitalism -- are foundational to any assessment of how the Internet has developed and is likely to develop."

Concerns about the online world often fixate on cutting-edge digital tech. But, as McChesney points out, "the criticism of out-of-control technology is in large part a critique of out-of-control commercialism. The loneliness, alienation, and unhappiness sometimes ascribed to the Internet are also associated with a marketplace gone wild."

Discourse about the Internet often proceeds as if digital technology has some kind of mind or will of its own. It does not.

For the most part, what has gone terribly wrong in digital realms is not about the technology. I often think of what Herbert Marcuse wrote in his 1964 book *One-Dimensional Man*: "The traditional notion of the 'neutrality' of technology can no longer be maintained. Technology as such cannot be isolated from the use to which it is put; the technological society is a system of domination which operates already in the concept and construction of techniques."

Marcuse saw the technological as fully enmeshed with the political in advanced industrial society, "the latest stage in the realization of a specific historical project -- namely, the experience, transformation, and organization of nature as the mere stuff of domination." He warned that the system's productivity and growth potential contained "technical progress within the framework of domination."

Huge corporations are now running roughshod over the Internet.

Fifty years later, McChesney's book points out: "The Internet and the broader digital revolution are not inexorably determined by technology; they are shaped by how society elects to develop them. . . . In really existing capitalism, the kind Americans actually experience, wealthy individuals and large corporations have immense political power that undermines the principles of democracy. Nowhere is this truer than in communication policy making."

Huge corporations are now running roughshod over the Internet. At the illusion-shattering core of *Digital Disconnect* are a pair of chapters on what corporate power has already done to the Internet -- the relentless commercialism that stalks every human online, gathering massive amounts of information to target people with ads; the decimation of privacy; the data mining and surveillance; the direct cooperation of Internet service providers, search engine companies, telecomm firms and other money-driven behemoths with the U.S. military and "national security" state; the ruthless insatiable drive, led by Apple, Google, Microsoft and other digital giants, to maximize profits.

In his new book, McChesney cogently lays out grim Internet realities. (Full disclosure: he's on the board of directors of an organization I founded, the Institute for Public Accuracy.) Compared to *Digital Disconnect,* the standard media critiques of the Internet are fairy tales.

Blowing away the corporate-fueled smoke, McChesney breaks through with insights like these:

- "The corporate media sector has spent much of the past 15 years doing everything in its immense power to limit the openness and egalitarianism of the Internet. Its survival and prosperity hinge upon making the system as closed and proprietary as possible, encouraging corporate and state surreptitious monitoring of Internet users and opening the floodgates of commercialism."

- "It is supremely ironic that the Internet, the much-ballyhooed champion of increased consumer power and cutthroat competition, has become one of the greatest generators of monopoly in economic history. Digital market concentration has proceeded far more furiously than in the traditional pattern found in other areas. . . As 'killer applications' have emerged, new digital industries have gone from competitive to oligopolistic to monopolistic at breakneck speeds."

- "Today, the Internet as a social medium and information system is the domain of a handful of colossal firms."

- "It is true that with the advent of the Internet many of the successful giants -- Apple and Google come to mind -- were begun by idealists who may have been uncertain whether they really wanted to be old-fashioned capitalists. The system in short order has whipped them into shape. Any qualms about privacy, commercialism, avoiding taxes, or paying low wages to Third World factory workers were quickly forgotten. It is not that the managers are particularly bad and greedy people -- indeed their individual moral makeup is mostly irrelevant -- but rather that the system sharply rewards some types of behavior and penalizes other types of behavior so that people either get with the program and internalize the necessary values or they fail."

- "The tremendous promise of the digital revolution has been compromised by capitalist appropriation and development of the Internet. In the great conflict between openness and a closed system of corporate profitability, the forces of capital have triumphed whenever an issue mattered to them. The Internet has been subjected to the capital-accumulation process, which has a clear logic of its own, inimical to much of the democratic potential of digital communication."

- "What seemed to be an increasingly open public sphere, removed from the world of commodity exchange, seems to be morphing into a private sphere of increasingly closed, proprietary, even monopolistic markets. The extent of this capitalist colonization of the Internet has not been as obtrusive as it might have been, because the vast reaches of cyberspace have continued to permit noncommercial utilization, although increasingly on the margins."

- "If the Internet is worth its salt, if it is to achieve the promise of its most euphoric celebrants and assuage the concerns of its most troubled skeptics, it has to be a force for raising the tide of democracy. That means it must help arrest the forces that promote inequality, monopoly, hypercommercialism, corruption, depoliticization, and stagnation."

- "Digital technologies may bring to a head, once and for all, the discrepancy between what a society could produce and what it actually does produce under capitalism. The Internet is the ultimate public good and is ideally suited for broad social development. It obliterates scarcity and is profoundly disposed toward democracy. And it is more than that. The new technologies are in the process of truly revolutionizing manufacturing, for example, making far less expensive, more efficient, environmentally sound, decentralized production possible. Under really existing capitalism, however, few of the prospective benefits may be developed -- not to mention spread widely. The corporate system will try to limit the technology to what best serves its purposes."

The huge imbalance of digital power now afflicting the Internet is a crucial subset of what afflicts the entirety of economic relations and political power in the United States. We have a profound, far-reaching fight on our hands, at a crossroads leading toward democracy or corporate monopoly. The future of humanity is at stake.

1. The author says the internet is now run by big businesses and has little to do with the original internet, which was a free-for-all. He believes this is a bad thing. What are three things you think big businesses—like Google, Apple, and Microsoft—have done to improve the internet?

2. Based on what you've learned about digital monopolies so far, do you think the author's critique of the internet and the companies that have become the biggest components of that space is fair? Explain.

"TO ADDRESS INEQUALITY, LET'S TAKE ON MONOPOLIES," BY BARRY LYNN AND KEVIN CARTY, FROM *COMMON DREAMS*, SEPTEMBER 22, 2017

Most Americans know that our country has become extremely unequal. They may not know that the richest 0.1% of Americans own as much wealth as the bottom 90%, or that the richest one percent took more than half of all income growth since 1979. But they know that the rich benefit more and more nowadays, while middle and working class families take home less and less.

Our team at the Open Markets Institute is dedicated to investigating and publicizing the radical concentrations of wealth — and of power — that are responsible for creating much of this extreme inequality. Through investigative journalism and historical and legal research we have shown that monopoly power is at the root of many of the most pressing injustices in America today—including degraded jobs, depressed entrepreneurship, financial instability, and the weakening of the economic and social fabric of communities all across the country.

Last month, our team of ten people was forced to leave our long-time home at a well-known Washington think tank. We were pushed out for expressing support for an antitrust decision against Google, a tech monopoly that is also one of that think tank's largest funders. Since then, we have re-established ourselves as an independent, non-profit organization that does not accept funding from any for-profit corporation. We are fully committed to continuing, and expanding, the groundbreaking reporting and research we have done for years.

The origins of America's monopoly problem today trace to the early 1980s, when an odd alliance of legal scholars and economists from the Right and Left pushed through a radical rethinking of America's traditional anti-monopoly philosophy. In stead of using antimonopoly law to protect our democratic institutions from concentrated power, they said we should aim only at making economic systems more "efficient," in order to better promote our "welfare" as "consumers."

In the decades since, every administration has embraced the tenets of this new "Chicago School" thinking, in the process abandoning the anti-monopoly policies which had helped underwrite the democracy and broad-based prosperity established during the New Deal era.

America's current economy bears the effects of that radical transformation. Four airlines control eighty percent of their market, two drug store chains dominate the pharmacy industry, and Google, Facebook, and Amazon each control nearly all of search, social media, and e-commerce online. The list goes on and on, with almost every industry in America — from agriculture to retail — having become highly concentrated.

This rapid rise in monopolization has increased inequality in all sorts of ways. Monopolistic businesses can charge people more for basic goods like health-care, transportation, and food. As Lina Khan, the Open Markets' Director of Legal Policy, and Sandeep Vaheesan explained recently in the Harvard Law and Policy Review, "monopoly pricing on goods and services... turns the disposable income of the many into capital gains, dividends, and executive compensation for the few."

Those same businesses also have more power to exploit their workers, because in a monopolized economy, there is less competition for the labor of the worker. In fact, one study from the University of Chicago found that individual wages today would be $14,000 higher per year (yes, $14,000!) if the economy had the same levels of competition as it had 30 years ago. It is no accident that Wal-Mart — the nation's biggest private employer — pays its workers less than a living wage, and crushes their unions when they try to organize. In many communities, workers have few places other than Wal-mart to sell their labor.

Monopoly power is very often brought to bear against the least advantaged in an already unequal society. Monopolistic meatpackers and farm operators subject their slaughterhouse workers, who are predominantly people of color, and their farm workers, who are predominantly immigrants, to exploitative labor conditions and stop them from forming unions to achieve better treatment. Monopoly, like the inequality it spurs, aggravates existing disparities.

Worse this inequality of economic power also promotes greater inequality in our political system. The same big businesses and big investors that raise prices, lower wages, and exploit the disadvantaged are also some of the most powerful actors in America's politics. Not only do they use their wealth to lobby lawmakers, fund academic researchers, and influence think tanks and policy experts, they also use their market power to pressure elected leaders, as when Aetna threatened to pull out of the Affordable Care Act exchanges unless the Obama administration approved its massive merger with Humana.

Our team looks forward to working with a broad coalition of allies to take on America's monopoly challenge, and put power back where it belongs — into the hands of workers, creators, families, and communities all across our great nation. This battle won't be easy, but the American people have taken on such concentrations of power before, and won. At Open Markets, we are confident that, working together, we will do it again.

1. The author notes that Google controls the majority of the internet's search business, Facebook controls most of our social media interactions, and Amazon is responsible for most of the e-commerce business. Based on the arguments laid out in the article, do you think these businesses are behaving in monopolistic ways, or do they merely appear to be monopolies because they have been chosen by consumers as the best of their kinds?

2. The author says that in addition to behaving in monopolistic ways, the businesses called out in the article also take advantage of their workers, who are typically low-income and disadvantaged, while also being big investors in the American political system. How do you think these behaviors influence the companies' monopolistic behaviors?

"NEUTRALITY BEGINS AT HOME: WHAT U.S. MAYORS CAN DO RIGHT NOW TO SUPPORT A NEUTRAL INTERNET," BY APRIL GLASER AND CORYNNE MCSHERRY, FROM *ELECTRONIC FRONTIER FOUNDATION*, JUNE 20, 2014

This weekend at the U.S. Conference of Mayors annual meeting in Dallas, some mayors will take a strong stand in support of net neutrality. According to an op-ed by Mayors Ed Lee of San Francisco and Ed Murray of Seattle, the city leaders are unveiling a resolution calling on the FCC to preserve an open Internet.

This is good and welcome news. The mayors get it: a free and open Internet is critically important for the health of U.S. cities. "The Internet has thrived because of its openness and equality of access," reads the mayors' op-ed. "It has spurred great innovation, while providing a level playing field for its users. It allows everyone the same chance to interact, to participate, to compete."

Here's some even better news: while the FCC may have a role to play in promoting and protecting a neutral Internet, city governments don't have to rely entirely on the FCC. In fact, there are two things Mayor Lee can do right now to protect the future of our open Internet: strongly support municipal wireless and light up the dark fiber that weaves its way under the city of San Francisco. And other mayors around the country have the same opportunity, if they've got the will to take it.

LIGHT UP THE DARK FIBER

"Dark fiber" refers to unused fiber optic lines already laid in cities around the country, intended to provide high speed, affordable Internet access to residents. In San Francisco alone, more than 110 miles of fiber optic cable run under the city. Only a fraction of that fiber network is being used.

And San Francisco isn't alone. Cities across the country have invested in laying fiber to connect nonprofits, schools, and government offices with high-speed Internet.

LIGHT UP COMPETITION

Community broadband is not a silver bullet for net neutrality. But it can help promote competition by doing one essential thing: offering people real alternatives.

In most U.S. cities there is only one option for high-speed broadband access. This is because in the early 2000s the FCC thought that competition alone would do the job of regulatory oversight, but instead Internet access providers consolidated to the point of no competition. And this lack of competition means that users can't vote with their feet when monopoly providers like Comcast or Verizon discriminate among Internet users in harmful ways. On the flipside, a lack of competition leaves these large Internet providers with little incentive to offer better service.

A non-neutral Internet, enabled by access monopolies, means that new businesses in cities could be crippled from reaching potential customers, as users are channeled toward incumbent websites and those in a special relationship with the Internet access providers. The result: a less diverse Internet and a weaker local economy.

REAL POLITICAL WILL CAN OVERCOME ARTIFICIAL POLITICAL AND LEGAL BARRIERS

Let's take a look at Chattanooga, Tennessee, a city that has better broadband than San Francisco. Chattanooga is home to one of the nation's least expensive, most robust municipally owned broadband networks. The city decided to build a high-speed network initially to meet the needs of the city's electric company that needed a way to monitor new equipment being installed through-out Chatanooga. Then, the local government learned that the cable companies would not be upgrading their Inter-net service fast enough to meet the city's needs. So the electric utility also became an ISP, and the residents of Chattanooga now have access to a gigabit (1,000 mega-bits) per second Internet connection. That's far ahead of the average US connection speed, which typically clocks in at 9.8 megabits per second.

And in Missouri, the city of Springfield crafted laws to navigate around state restrictions on municipal broad-band. Now Springfield provides its own access service, SpringNet, and is offering businesses high capacity fiber Internet service.

Unfortunately, many cities have faced serious barriers to their efforts to light up dark fiber or extend existing networks. Take Washington D.C., where the city's fiber is bound up in a non-compete contract with Comcast, keeping the network from serving businesses and residents.

San Francisco doesn't have the same kind of contractual barriers that D.C. has, but the city's network is still under-used. San Francisco's fiber connects important institutions like libraries, schools, public housing, and public wi-fi projects. However, according to Harvard University researcher Susan Crawford, San Francisco "has not yet cracked the nut of alternative community residential or business fiber access."

Here, too, San Francisco is not alone. Right now 89 U.S. cities provide residents with high-speed home Internet. And dozens of cities across the country have the infrastructure, such as dark fiber, to either offer high-speed broadband Internet to residents or lease out the fiber to new Internet access providers to bring more competition to the marketplace. So the infrastructure to provide municipal alternatives is there in many places — we just need the will and savvy to make it a reality that works.

That said, the most outrageous barrier is a legal one: state laws, promoted by powerful incumbent Internet access providers, that impede competition by imposing restrictions on cities' ability to grow broadband networks. Twenty states currently have laws that restrict or discourage municipalities and communities from building their own broadband networks.

Fortunately, the FCC has said it will challenge these laws. But the FCC can't create the political commitment to actually making community broadband happen. That's up to us.

ALL HANDS ON DECK

It's going to take a constellation of solutions to keep our Internet open. But where those options don't depend on regulators and legislators in D.C., we don't need to wait.

Whether it's lighting up dark fiber or starting a municipal broadband network, we can tell our elected officials to take action to protect our open Internet.

That's why we're calling for all hands on deck. In cities with dark fiber, like San Francisco, it's time to light it up. Mayor Ed Lee knows the importance of an open and free Internet. San Francisco is renowned for being home to some of the most innovative Internet companies and startups in the world. The city should be a leader in community broadband as well.

But what's really exciting is that this is one area where we call all be leaders. We can all organize locally and urge our city officials to support municipal and community broadband projects. To help spur that work, EFF will be sharing more ideas and tools for activism in the coming weeks.

And remember: the FCC is seeking public comment about how to craft new network neutrality rules. Visit DearFCC.org right now and make sure the agency hears us loud and clear: we're not going to let a few Internet access providers decide the future of our open Internet.

1. Net neutrality is seen as a type of antitrust action because it treats all online content equally and keeps internet service providers from deciding what consumers can access. How do you think this helps prevent digital monopolies?

2. As noted in the article, many US cities only have one option for high-speed internet access because many service providers have merged over the years, leading to fewer providers overall. The authors note that this, coupled with other digital monopolies, would lead to a less diverse online environment and a weaker economy. What are some ways that limited service options could lead to these results?

CHAPTER 5

WHAT THE MEDIA SAY

The media has long been opposed to monopolies and in favor of antitrust actions. The media has fought against monopolies not only because they hurt the public, but because there are monopolies that could hurt the media—like Google and Facebook, which take up the majority of the online advertising business and hurt media companies that rely on ads to help pay for their content. As you read the following opinions about digital trusts, you'll be asked to think about the arguments being made and whether the companies accused of digital monopolies are guilty based on the evidence provided.

"THE EU'S OBSESSION WITH GOOGLE SHOWS HOW LITTLE IT UNDERSTANDS THE DIGITAL ECONOMY," BY DAVID GLANCE, FROM *THE CONVERSATION*, NOVEMBER 30, 2014

The Parliament of the European Union last week voted to call on member states and the European Commission to investigate the operation of search engines in Europe to ensure "a balanced, fair and open internet search structure".

Although the official text of the resolution doesn't mention Google specifically by name, the message was clearly aimed at the company that claims 93% of the European search market. The Parliament called on the EC to "consider proposals aimed at unbundling search engines from other commercial services".

The EU's aim in all of this was to try and bring about what it considered a "level playing field" that allows competition from other search providers. It is also concerned, because Google's competitors have voiced these concerns, that Google is using search as a way of unfairly driving traffic to its own services, in preference to the competition.

The recommendations go even further however and try to address the issues of how search itself should operate in order "that indexation, evaluation, presentation and ranking by search engines must be unbiased and transparent".

This effectively means that the EU would determine how Google's search algorithms would work and what results should be returned by any given search. Something that would clearly be beyond the EU and impossible to implement without severely limiting Google in the process.

It seems that the European Competition Commissioner Margretha Vestager will be unswayed by the non-binding vote. Her spokesperson stated that how the Commissioner applies the law will be as a result of the Commission's investigations and not influenced by politics. It is certainly not clear that she would advocate splitting Google in two, as it would be both extremely hard to achieve and ultimately, unlikely to result in the ends the EU were striving for.

THE EU'S VISION OF A SINGLE DIGITAL MARKET

The issue of search engines was only one small part of the EU Parliament's plans for a European consumer-friendly single digital market. Overall, the efficiencies that they imagine this market will bring to Europe are a massive Euro 260 billion a year. But here again, the EU will face significant challenges if it believes that it is going to bring this innovation about without the dominant players.

The Parliament recognises that in Europe, the "app economy alone is expected to triple its revenue from 2013 to 2018, creating 3 million jobs in the same period". But who controls this "app economy"? Google, through Android, and Apple.

It also talks about the need to "foster the mass adoption of cloud computing in Europe, as it constitutes a powerful driver for the growth of the European economy". Again, who is the dominant player in cloud computing? Amazon.

Wherever Europe turns, if it is going to implement a digital market, it will have to do so with the help of dominant technological players and they all happen to be American.

REMEMBERING THE PAST.
THE EU VS MICROSOFT

Even if the EU is reluctant to accept the future, it should at least remember its past. The last time it tried to regulate what they perceived as a monopoly in the technological space, was its long battle with Microsoft. In that case, the EU distilled the entire significance of the PC revolution to Microsoft's media player and its Internet browser, Internet Explorer.

The EU ruled that Microsoft should provide versions of Windows that "unbundled" the Windows Media Player and offered consumers a choice of browser. Ultimately, this was always going to be a drop in the ocean in terms of its impact on Microsoft, consumers, and the digital economy as a whole. More importantly, the focus on these technologies was rapidly rendered redundant by the rise of mobile phones and Microsoft's monopoly being made largely moot as mobile became the dominant platform.

TECHNOLOGY, POLITICS, AND LAW

What the case against Microsoft showed that the technology landscape fundamentally can't be shaped by politics or the law. Firstly there is a lack of understanding of what the landscape actually is, and secondly, nobody knows, especially lawmakers and politicians, how technology should best be directed for equitable and maximum benefit for all. Finally, technology moves too quickly for committee-driven processes to keep up.

The EU's lack of understanding of the digital economy is evident from the language they have used in their recommendations on the single digital market. Even the concept of a single digital market itself is more of a marketing strategy intended to mask the real agenda of trying to protect and grow European digital companies in the face of US dominance.

SWEAT THE SMALL STUFF AND LEAVE THE REST TO OTHERS

There is no doubt that there are real issues to tackle with the digital economy in terms of privacy, intellectual property and yes, even the blatant misuse of market strength. The EU should perhaps focus on the things they can actually change to promote the development of European companies that could compete with the current leaders. Funding and promoting education, research and development are all solid building blocks to start this, not artificially trying to handicap the competition.

1. In the European Union (EU), at the time the article was written, Google took up 93 percent of the EU's online search traffic. The EU felt that this was a problem and wanted to created a "balanced, fair and open internet search structure." Based on your knowledge of online searches and the options available, do you think in this instance Google's monopoly was caused by Google, or by the consumers in the EU?

2. The author suggests that the EU is less concerned with Google's control of the search market, but of how it promotes its own products in search over all other similar products. Do you think this is a valid concern? Does it make what Google is doing monopolistic, or is it a fair business practice?

"GOOGLE FINE SHOWS EU 'WAY AHEAD' OF US ON REINING IN MASSIVE CORPORATIONS," BY JAKE JOHNSON, FROM *COMMON DREAMS*, JUNE 27, 2017

In a move commentators characterized as a "promising" step in the direction of regulating and reining in large and powerful tech firms, the European Commission on Tuesday slapped Google with a $2.7 billion fine for violating antitrust rules and "abus[ing] its market dominance."

Specifically, the commission noted in a press release, Google was penalized for using its leverage to give "an illegal advantage" to its own shopping service, which had the effect of boxing out potential competition.

Matt Stoller, a fellow at New America's Open Markets Program, responded by saying that the EU's decision to take action against Google provides a stark contrast to the inaction of American regulators, who have in recent years done relatively little to prevent large companies from merging and drowning out competitors.

"This $2.7 [billion] fine is not a parking ticket for Google," Stoller wrote. "It opens the door to civil suits. And Google has to change its behavior."

Leadership on curbing monopoly power has been in Europe, not the U.S., "for some time," Stoller added. "American antitrust authorities are so pathetic as to be irrelevant."

The fine—the largest ever leveled against a single company by the EU in an antitrust case—marks the end of a seven-year investigation into Google's practices.

The commission further explained its decision:

> The Commission Decision does not object to the design of Google's generic search algorithms or to demotions as such, nor to the way that Google displays or organises its search results pages (e.g. the display of a box with comparison shopping results displayed prominently in a rich, attractive format). It objects to the fact that Google has leveraged its market dominance in general internet search into a separate market, comparison shopping. Google abused its market dominance as a search engine to promote its own comparison shopping service in search results, whilst demoting those of rivals.

"What Google has done is illegal under [European Union] antitrust rules. It denied other companies the chance to compete on the merits and to innovate. And most importantly, it denied European consumers a genuine choice of services and the full benefits of innovation," said European Commissioner for Competition Margrethe Vestager in a statement.

In an op-ed for the *Guardian*, journalist Nils Pratley echoed Stoller's argument.

The E.U. regulators' "consumer-friendly action... should be applauded," he wrote, adding that the move could have "far-reaching consequences."

"The wonder is that U.S. regulators, who once upon a time had an honourable record of acting against powerful monopolists, have been so supine with the technology giants," Pratley concluded.

1. Google was fined by the EU for using its search engine to promote its own shopping service over other online retailers and violating antitrust laws. Based on what the author presents, do you agree with the EU's decision?
2. Based on everything you've read, do you think what Google did was against the EU's antitrust laws? Do you think that a nondigital business would have the same ability to act the way Google did?

"AS TECH GIANTS THREATEN DEMOCRACY, CALLS GROW FOR NEW ANTI-MONOPOLY MOVEMENT," BY JAKE JOHNSON, FROM *COMMON DREAMS*, SEPTEMBER 1, 2017

A major Washington-based think tank's decision to fire a prominent Google critic earlier this week brought to the surface the massive and "disturbing" influence large tech companies have on political debate in the

U.S., leading many analysts and lawmakers to call for the creation of an anti-monopoly movement to take on the threat consolidated corporate power poses to the democratic process.

As Brian Fund and Hamza Shaban note in an analysis for *the Washington Post*, "funding of think tanks is just one way Silicon Valley is expanding its influence in Washington." Tech giants like Google, Amazon, Facebook, and Apple are also "regularly setting records in their spending on lobbying and are pushing as many as 100 issues—or more—every year."

Such clout has allowed tech companies to exert enormous influence on economic policy, and on the terms of political discussion.

A stark indication of this influence was on display Wednesday, when Barry Lynn, a prominent critic of corporate power, was ousted from the influential think tank New America for praising the European Union's decision to fine Google for "abusing its market dominance."

As a consequence of this experience, Lynn spearheaded the creation of Citizens Against Monopoly, a project devoted to documenting and warning against "the dangers of concentrated private power."

"[S]ince the early days of the Reagan administration, power over almost all forms of economic activity in America has been steadily concentrated in fewer and fewer hands," Lynn notes in an op-ed for *the Washington Post.* "This includes retail and transportation. It includes pharmaceuticals and farming. It includes almost every corner of the internet."

This consolidation of private power is not only a threat to "our economic well-being," Lynn observes. It is also a dire threat to democracy itself.

"Wherever you work, whatever you do, your livelihood, and your liberties are every day more at risk as long as we allow a few giant corporations—especially in online commerce—to continue to extend their reach into and over the world of ideas," Lynn concluded.

Matt Stoller, formerly a fellow at New America who has joined Lynn at Citizens Against Monopoly, argued in a piece for Buzzfeed that corporate consolidation "lets a small group of people exercise control over a much larger group, which results in both extremes of wealth inequality and extremes of political corruption."

Judging by recent polling data—and the popularity of lawmakers like Sen. Bernie Sanders (I-Vt.), who made concentration of corporate power a central issue of his 2016 presidential campaign—Americans agree with Lynn and Stoller: 71 percent believe the economy is "rigged," and most believe that corporations have too much power.

"It is time for citizens in America and all over the world to stand up to the bullies in our society. It is time to look to the real governors and regulators in America and around the world, the monopolists," Stoller concluded. "It's been more than 70 years since we've seen a broad-based citizens movement against the power of monopoly. It's long past time for one."

Following Lynn's firing, several prominent progressive lawmakers expressed support for the Citizens Against Monopoly effort, including Sen. Elizabeth Warren (D-Mass.) and Rep. John Conyers (D-Mich.).

On Twitter, Conyers declared: "Americans are fed up with monopolies rigging our economy and politics."

1. The author notes that a group, Citizens Against Monopoly, believes that business monopolies are not only bad for consumers, but for democracy. Based on the article you just read, and the previous articles in this chapter, list three reasons digital monopolies could be bad for the political landscape.

2. The author says that many citizens believe that corporations have too much power. Based on the evidence presented in the article, do you think this is related to monopolies? Why or why not?

CHAPTER 6

WHAT ORDINARY PEOPLE SAY

The average citizen is against monopolies. We know this because people continue to choose to do business with new companies and to demand better treatment from large corporations. Cab-riders first chose to ride with Uber, but as companies like Lyft and Juno appeared on the scene, they've chosen to use some or all the available options to make their lives easier. People get streaming video not from one source, but from many. And they switch cellphone carriers and cable companies whenever a better deal is available. As you read the following articles, you'll learn how consumers feel about digital monopolies and what they think should be done to protect their rights online.

"PEOPLE'S ECONOMIES VS CORPORATE CONTROL: FIRST COMMODIFICATION, THEN FINANCIALIZATION, NOW DEMONETIZATION," BY VANDANA SHIVA, FROM *COMMON DREAMS*, DECEMBER 5, 2016

Ever since the Corporate Form was "invented" - in its earliest avatar as the collective East India Companies - those who have ruled via corporation have found innovative "means" new to extract wealth from the earth and people, leaving both poorer in a zero-sum "game".

During The Raj - Company Raj - extraction was carried out through *Lagaan* - taxation on land & agriculture. Between 1765 to 1815,the Company is recorded to have pirated **£ 18 Million annually from India**. 50 % of the produce was taken as Lagaan, creating famines like the Great Bengal Famine.

The Company destroyed the people's circular, sustainable and just economies - in which 70% of the value of what rural areas produced circulated in the village economy - and replaced them with linear, extractive economies, where most wealth produced in India went to enrich England, bleeding India.

In recent years, the corporate empire has found new instruments of extraction, with patents and (what should be called) 'capitalisation', being two prominent ones. The Chemical/Biotech/Seed Industry "innovated" and "invented" patents on life and patents on seeds, as a means to extract profits from farmers.

The second instrument - capitalisation - the financialisation of the economy is equally perverse. It has punished real people, marginalised the real wealth that people produce in real economies, and rewarded only the capital-ists. The capital economy has become 70 times bigger than there real economy. The Wall street Crash of 2008 was a result of the creation of this global casino. We were protected, insulated in India because our economy was still real.

The concentration of the worlds wealth in the hands of the 1% is a consequence of patent-isation, capital-isation, and the digit-isation of our lives. The latest bait and switch being used by globalised corporate power, to worm its way into the households of India, is the demonising or "Demonetisation" (as it has been "Hash!-*tagged*") of Indian Currency.

The "demonetisation" of the India's economy of more that 1 billion people at the stroke of midnight on 8th November 2016 is the next gamble of the corporate empire to steal people's wealth, lock it away behind an encryption key, and shut down people's economies overnight leaving only the parts of the economy willing to indulge the payment-gateway-keeper. Naspers Group is that gatekeeper for Digital India.

More than 90% of India functions on cash to sustain the people's economy. Cash is a neutral form of money, one person's hard earned money is as potent as another's; there are no "AMEX Black" ₹1000 notes, yet. 86% of all the currency was made illegal overnight, but that is a de-humanised number. If a chaiwallah (who does not yet find himself dictating monetary policy), accumulates the change he earns, exchanging for ₹100, then ₹500, working his way up to a collection of ₹1000 notes as his savings. He prefers the ₹1000 because they are easier to carry and secure, especially since he does not have a bank account - because he has no address - because he can't afford to rent an address and has not inherited one. At the stroke of midnight on 8th November 2016, this chai-but-no-house-wallah disappeared from the economy. A Nescafé machine will replace him.

The purest currency in people's economies is life, it is love, it is community, and communion, it is trust. That is why the most civilised societies, when measured in terms of their humanity, happiness and well being, are societies based on barter. When cash becomes the currency of exchange, it can still build community through face to face transactions. People's Economies are based on solidarity.

Just as patents on seeds were an illegitimate attempt to criminalise farmers by making seed saving illegal, "#demonetisation" is an illegitimate attempt to criminalise the people's economy which is 80% of India's real economy.

That this is the aim is clear from the statement of the man who became the richest in the world through patents and the digital economy -Bill Gates.

As he stated in his speech for the 'NITI-Lectures series: Transforming India' in the presence of PM Narendra Modi and his Cabinet colleagues,"the government's bold move to demonetise high-value denominations and replace them with new notes with high security features was an important step to move away from the shadow economy to a more transparent economy."

Gates said digital transactions would rise dramatically, and, in the next several years, India would become one of the most digitised economies not just by size, but percentage as well.

The "Pirate of Silicon Valley" has just declared the vibrant community based Swadeshi economy of the people of India a "shadow" economy, just because it is beyond the reach of his digital monopoly. We are not shadows of your empire, Mr Gates. We are hard working, honest people who still know how to trust and share, who have community and real creativity to run and sustain our economy. Transparency as defined by you as the asymmetric power of the financial and digital world over people, to take control of our wealth, our wellbeing, our lives, our freedoms.

It is the end of being in a relationship of trust with a person you know in your local economy, and see face to face. It is the end of people being transparent to each other as human beings. It is not financial transparency either that is supposed to end "Black Money". You and Microsoft are part of the "Black Economy". A 2012 report from the US Senate found that Microsoft's use of offshore subsidiaries enabled it to avoid taxes of $4.5 billion, a sum greater than the Bill and Melinda Gates Foundation annual grant making ($3.6 billion in 2014). You want to teach us transparency?

How Piracy Opens Doors for Windows, an *LA Times* article dated 9th April 2006 quotes Bill Gates:

"Although about 3 million computers get sold every year in China, people don't pay for the software. Someday they will, though," Gates told an audience at the University of Washington. "And as long as they're going to steal it, we want them to steal ours. They'll get sort of addicted, and then we'll somehow figure out how to collect sometime in the next decade."

Gates' payment portals are here to collect.

In 1857 we drove out the first Corporation that ruled the world, the East India Company. In 1947 we drove out the British who controlled 80% of the territories of the world. Our determination to defend our economic freedoms, economic democracy and economic sovereignty through Swadeshi is stronger than ever. The need for Swadeshi has never been greater. We will defend and sustain our people's economies -by the people, of the people, for the people, against the assault of the corporate economy run by the corporations, for the corporations.

1. The author declares that Microsoft runs a digital monopoly and that the people of India are its latest victims. She suggests that Microsoft is trying to take over the Indian economy, which is based largely in cash and not digital or credit card payments, and that this would hurt local businesses. Why do you think this is a problem in India, based on the author's writing?

2. The author quotes Bill Gates several times, implying that the quotes show Gates's desire to create a monopoly. Do you think those quotes show an intention to create a monopoly?

"THE PUBLIC SAYS: BREAK BIG MEDIA MONOPOLIES AND HELP NEW JOURNALISM PROJECTS," BY DES FREEDMAN, FROM *THE CONVERSATION*, APRIL 1, 2015

So far, any analysis of the role of the media in the forthcoming election has focused overwhelmingly on the leaders' debates and on the "horse-race" coverage. But very little has been said about the crucial issue that underpins the agenda-setting power of news organisations: the domination of our media by a handful of giant corporations.

Now, a new poll conducted by YouGov for the Media Reform Coalition has proved what campaigners have long been arguing: that there is strong public support for measures to tackle media concentration, to make proprietors more accountable to their audiences and their journalists and to secure funds for new forms of local and investigative journalism.

Nearly three-quarters – 74% – of those polled said they support controls on media ownership, while a substantial minority, some 41%, believe that existing rules should be strengthened by setting fixed limits on the amount of media any one proprietor or entity can own. Similarly, 74% believe that media owners should be required to have UK residency and pay full UK taxes while 61% would support compulsory rules or structures (such as genuinely independent editorial boards) in order to limit the influence of owners over editorial output.

Peter Oborne's resignation from *The Daily Telegraph* in protest at the title's downplaying of HSBC's involvement in tax avoidance schemes in order not to jeopardise its advertising with the bank seems also to have influenced public opinion. Some 64% of those polled would support an inquiry into the relationship between news organisations and advertisers. Only 7% said they were unconcerned about the rise of "branded content" and the breakdown of the distinction between editorial and commercial output.

When asked whether they would support a levy on the profits of social media and pay TV companies to support new providers of independent journalism, 51% agreed and only a tiny minority, 9% of those polled, rejected the idea. Given that Google has already agreed to a £52m "contribution" to support a "digital publishing innovation fund", this is not as controversial as it sounds. It's high time that a British politician should make this demand of Google and other internet companies.

BOTTLING IT

But which of our leading politicians will dare to challenge the power of organisations whose support they believe will be crucial to securing votes? Perhaps it is worth remembering that Ed Miliband's popularity soared both when he threatened to "break up" the Murdoch empire and when he accused the *Daily Mail* of smearing his late father as a "man who hated Britain".

Indeed, cracks have started to emerge in relation to media ownership. The Greens recently announced that a commitment to limit ownership in any individual media market to a maximum of 20% would feature in their manifesto. Meanwhile the Lib Dems have now called for an end to the ability of ministers to rule on media takeovers. This was a clear reference to News Corporation's attempted acquisition of BSkyB, a deal that was waved through by then culture secretary Jeremy Hunt before it was withdrawn once the phone hacking scandal blew up.

Perhaps it is significant that the Labour peer, David Puttnam, used his recent speech to the Media Trust to criticise David Cameron for "bottling" his chance to force proprietors to accept a genuinely independent form of regulation and to condemn the complicity between politicians and the media, a situation that was made worse, according to *The Guardian* by the "moral airlock that allows companies to prioritise profits over broader values".

Lord Puttnam is right to focus on the underlying structures of media power that are at the heart of the unethical and ungratifying behaviour of too much of our media. Revelations of widespread phone hacking at the *Daily Mirror* and allegations about what would appear to be a degraded editorial policy at the world's most popular online title, DailyMail.com, are just some of the more recent manifestations of the abuse of this power.

The point is that influential media organisations in highly concentrated online and offline markets distort democratic debate. They routinely privilege issues and agendas that suit the interests of proprietors and advertisers. They foster questionable relationships between public officials and media barons. And they put (what appears to be) irresistible pressure on compliant politicians – who are increasingly nervous to upset such influential gatekeepers.

How can we expect fearless and robust coverage of climate change, financial scandals, austerity policies, policing, immigration and foreign affairs when so much of our established media are in hock to vested interests? And how can expect coverage of the election to go beyond both an obsession with personalities and the issues that party leaders want us to focus on without first challenging – and ultimately changing – the intimate relationships between the media and the political establishment it is supposed to hold to account?

Media power ought not to shape this election – instead it should be a central policy question that features in the election. Who will be brave enough to raise this the loudest?

1. In the United Kingdom, 74 percent of citizens say they'd support controls on media ownership, and 51 percent say they'd like to see taxes on social media and cable TV companies to pay for independent journalism projects. Based on what you've read, do you think that this is a reaction to media monopolies? Explain.

2. Previous articles in this book have suggested that there's a connection between large, monopolistic corporations and political power. Do you think limiting media ownership will break up the power certain companies and owners have on political issues?

"THE DIGITAL ECONOMY IS NO LEVELER, IT'S A SOURCE OF INEQUALITY," BY ANDREW WHITE, FROM *THE CONVERSATION*, JANUARY 26, 2015

When we think about income and wealth inequalities we are tempted to lay blame on the old way of doing things. In Capital in the Twenty-First Century, Thomas Piketty picks out inherited money as a driver of unsustainable disparities between the global rich and poor. Oxfam recently pinpointed the high-profit finance and pharmaceutical industries as engines of inequality that distribute wealth to the wealthy.

This view is consistent with those who place their faith in the digital economy as some kind of solution. It is held up as an alternative to traditional forms of economic activity, and one which can generate sustainable growth and narrow inequality. Lower barriers of entry into its markets ("anyone can start a business on the internet!") is said to widen opportunities and lead to a more equitable distribution of wealth.

It is for this reason that many politicians and academics continue to advocate the aggressive expansion of the digital economy, especially into areas which have not witnessed much of this type of economic activity. Sadly, it's not quite as simple as that.

CREATIVE LICENSE

The expansion of the digital economy has gone hand-in-hand with the growth of the creative industries. The UK's pioneering development of policy on the creative industries in the late 1990s was predicated partly on the desire to exploit the intellectual property generated by burgeoning digital technology. That applied particularly to those single operators and small businesses that proliferated in the cultural and creative sectors.

Similar policies have been used in countries at varying levels of development in the early years of the 21st century. Look at the UN's enthusiastic promotion of the creative economy, and its suggestion that these kind of structural reforms could work in both the developed world and in emerging markets. This explains why much research on developmental economics focuses on narrowing the so-called digital divide in order to give more equal access to a global economic system which promises prosperity for all.

But what if the problem is the digital economy itself rather than our incapacity to fully exploit the opportunities it seemingly presents? The first chapter of Michael Lewis's book *Flash Boys* opens with a story about construction workers on a project to lay a tunnel for fibre-optic cables as straight as they possibly could, even if this involved digging through mountains or river beds. The reason: to connect financial exchanges in New York and Chicago by the shortest possible route and give the operators a crucial few milliseconds advantage when processing transactions.

A huge amount of money is required to carry out such projects, and to buy the supercomputers that can manipulate the data and run the trading programs. It starts to look like a rigged game and it is difficult to see how a digital economy in which financial speculation is so prominent can reduce inequality.

STUCK IN THE MIDDLE WITH YOU

There are undoubtedly other sectors of the digital economy where lower barriers of entry do encourage smaller operators. The early development of search engines and social networking were characterised by experimentation by single operators or small groups of people, sometimes students, at home or at university. This pioneering image of isolated entrepreneurs developing great companies from scratch goes hand-in-hand with radical sounding rhetoric about taking on vested interests.

In this worldview, cutting out the middle man, a superfluous type of employee who will not move with the times, is seen as a demonstrably good thing. Thus, taxi drivers who complain about having their business taken away by Uber are often described as inflexible and prone to over-charging. But the middle-man has not disappeared in the digital economy; they have just got richer.

Think of the music industry. Online stores have resulted in the loss of many jobs as a result of physical record stores closing down. However, our changing habits have not cut out the middle-man. We buy most of our music from intermediaries like Apple. Even record labels, seemingly superfluous to the online music industry, continue to flourish.

In other words, while the poorer middle-men – record store assistants, or taxi drivers – have been ruthlessly squeezed, wealthier intermediaries continue to prosper. Even the supposedly lower barriers to entry in these industries have not prevented monopolies emerging in online markets in a way that is not as prominent in markets offline.

A ROLE FOR UNIVERSITIES

It would be easy to finish this piece with a long list of proposed solutions to these inequities. But what is really needed is the necessary intellectual work of persuading wider society that the digital economy does indeed pose problems. This is not helped by the sense that higher education, one of the best placed sectors to lead this debate, is not always up to this task.

While the views that are expressed in this article are shared by many in this sector, It is often difficult to seek institutional support for research in this area when the coalition government's policy of requiring humanities-based schools and departments to be financially self-sustaining has driven many of them into the arms of big business or into partnership with STEM (Science, Technology, Engineering and Mathematics) colleagues who might not be as interested in a critical examination of the foundations of the digital economy.

Many of these solutions involve digital technology, with big data being the latest whose application promises to address various social and economic woes. How welcome it would be if funding bodies could also increase the number of schemes which ask why the rapid growth of the digital economy over the past two decades has failed both to reduce inequality and save us from the most severe financial crisis since the 1930s.

1. The internet is supposed to be an equalizer, according to the author, making it easier for people to start online businesses and compete.

199

However, this has not been the case, and the author suggests that digital monopolies are to blame. Based on the evidence provided, do you think the internet provides more opportunities for small businesses, or is it more susceptible to monopolies?

2. The author notes that only certain people benefit from digital businesses, and that typical blue-collar workers are the ones who get cut out of the profits. This, as you've learned from previous articles, is also something that monopolies do. In this instance, do you think the author is pointing to a problem with monopolies, or with online business in general? Give an example from the article to explain your answer.

"ARE US ANTITRUST REGULATORS GIVING SILICON VALLEY'S 'FREE' APPS A FREE PASS?" BY JOHN NEWMAN, FROM *THE CONVERSATION*, AUGUST 29, 2016

Judging by the political winds, Silicon Valley seems headed for a showdown with antitrust regulators.

For the first time since 1988, the Democratic Party's platform includes stronger antitrust enforcement, while leading liberals have singled out Google, Apple and Facebook for holding too much market power.

Republicans considered (but ultimately rejected) inserting stronger antitrust language in their party platform, and standard-bearer Donald Trump has a famously frosty relationship with Silicon Valley, favoring heavier taxation and forcing Apple to shift manufacturing to the U.S.

Those expecting a showdown, however, may be disappointed. That's because antitrust regulators and U.S. judges tend to believe that products that don't cost a dime are beyond their purview. And that's how most of Silicon Valley's products are marketed these days. Facebook's slogan reassures: "It's free and always will be." Google claims: "One free account gets you into everything Google." And Apple has an entire section of its App Store devoted to "free apps."

Drawing on my experiences as a former Department of Justice antitrust attorney, I've argued that U.S. antitrust laws are in fact broad enough to include these products – which are hardly "free." Unfortunately, however, as my analysis of the history of enforcement in these markets shows, the trend in the U.S. has been away from antitrust oversight.

EVERYTHING IS 'FREE'

We live in an increasingly "free" world.

Ours is a world where vast libraries of information and content are available at the click of a button or tap of a screen – and all of it is (seemingly) free. Google search, Twitter, Instagram, Pokémon Go: all free.

If these products are freely available, what room is there for antitrust, a body of law often understood as

201

focused on protecting consumers from artificially high monopoly prices?

Prominent judge (and antitrust legend) Robert Bork, for example, contended that search engines cannot be liable under antitrust laws because they are "free to consumers."

U.S. antitrust enforcers appear, for the most part, to agree with Bork. Since the early days of the internet, "free" digital products have largely escaped scrutiny.

GIVING 'FREE' A FREE PASS

The first antitrust case targeting free digital products was also the most famous. At the outset of the 1990s Microsoft trial, the Department of Justice initially pursued a predatory pricing theory: Microsoft, it alleged, "set a zero price for its browser for the purpose of depriving Netscape of revenue and protecting [Microsoft's] operating system monopoly."

In other words, the DOJ at first argued that offering a product for free doesn't excuse a company from antitrust liability. But the government subsequently dropped this theory on appeal. It is unclear why it did so, though a 1993 Supreme Court ruling had made any predatory pricing lawsuit virtually impossible to win. Perhaps the added difficulty of convincing an appellate judge that "free" was illegal simply caused the government to focus on more core aspects of the appeal.

In any case, ever since then the courts have continued to be skeptical of that type of argument.

One of the earliest antitrust lawsuits against Google was brought by a private company that alleged Google was exploiting its free online search service in an anti-competitive manner. The complaint was dismissed in 2007 by a court reasoning that antitrust law does not "concern itself with competition in the provision of free services."

In 2008, the Federal Trade Commission allowed Google to acquire online advertising giant DoubleClick. Only one of the five commissioners voted to block the merger, pointing out that the acquisition would give Google access to a wealth of user data that could tip the market for search advertising (closely related to the market for free online search) further in favor of Google.

Four years later, the agency unanimously approved Facebook's acquisition of free photo-sharing network Instagram, though many industry observers concluded that Facebook was paying a massive premium to stave off competition from its upstart rival.

And the next year, the agency voted (again unanimously) to close its investigation into Google's conduct in the free online search market, despite a leaked staff report identifying harm to consumers caused by the search giant.

All in all, "free" products seem to warrant a free pass from U.S. antitrust laws. But not so in other jurisdictions.

Russia's Federal Antitrust Service in August issued a US$6.8 million fine against Google for abusing its market position with Android by favoring its own digital services over those of rivals.

Earlier this summer, the European Union issued its third statement of objection to Google, meaning Google could face up to three antitrust charges relating to its free search service, free smartphone operating system and its search-advertising platform. And Germany's antitrust regulator is currently investigating Facebook's privacy practices.

'FREE' MARKETS ARE STILL MARKETS

Why have international enforcement agencies responded so differently than those in the U.S.? Are they just unfairly targeting successful U.S. firms, as some (including Treasury Secretary Jacob Lew) claim? Or do they see something that we've missed?

U.S. antitrust law is uniquely devoted to a strain of economics often called "price theory." Beginning in the 1970s, price theory came to dominate antitrust law and scholarship.

Price theory (no surprise) focuses on prices. Supposedly, price theory uses price as a synechdoche to represent all aspects of competition. But in fact, businesses compete not just on price but also on quality, innovation, branding and other product attributes.

Yet U.S. antitrust regulators and courts have traditionally focused heavily on price competition. When products are "free" (or, more accurately, "zero-price"), they simply slip under the antitrust radar.

Such, I would argue, was the case in the broadcast radio industry, which has long offered a service "free" to listeners.

In 1996, Congress passed the Telecommunications Act, which removed a longstanding limit on how many stations a single entity can own. A frenzy of mergers and acquisitions followed.

U.S. antitrust enforcement agencies screened these transactions for possible harm to competition but only looked for higher prices to advertisers, neglecting to analyze potential harm to listeners. Most of the mergers were cleared without objection. The resulting lack of competition in many regions means that radio listeners now pay more – by listening to more ads – in exchange for the product they want.

That result should come as no surprise. Listeners may not pay for broadcast radio with money, but they do pay with attention. At its core, this is a prototypical market exchange, as contract law has long recognized.

THERE'S (STILL) NO SUCH THING AS A FREE LUNCH

In fact, the very idea of for-profit businesses giving consumers products for free ought to seem odd.

When it comes to the marketplace, as Milton Friedman famously quipped, "There is no free lunch." The internet did not destroy firms' profit motive. It also did not eliminate the cost of making products: Try recreating Google's "Street View" feature without funding for a global fleet of cars, cameras and drivers, not to mention banks of servers for processing and data storage.

Companies like Google, though innovative, are not in the business of giving away their products for free – and they are surely not immune from the temptation to stifle competition.

"Free" isn't really free. Consumers pay for "free" products with attention to ads and with personal information. Each time you log on or run a search, you pay with your time (that fraction of a second your eye spends darting over to the "Lose belly fat with this one weird trick!" ad) or information (letting Google know that you are thinking about buying a new sofa or suffer from anxiety disorder). These are commercial exchanges, even if consumers – and consumer protection laws – often fail to recognize them as such.

Antitrust laws are meant to safeguard marketplace competition, but doing so effectively requires protecting all markets, not just those with obvious prices.

This is why I believe U.S. enforcement agencies and courts ought to follow the lead set by their international peers and withdraw the free pass enjoyed by businesses supplying "free" products.

1. The author points out that a prominent antitrust judge said that search engines can't be bound by antitrust laws because they are "free to consumers." Do you think this is a reasonable standard?

2. Price-fixing or price intimidation is one of the marks of a monopolistic company. Since free services can't do this, do you think they are still capable of monopolistic behavior? Explain using two examples from your reading.

"SMASH THE MACHINE: DIGITAL MONOPOLIES HAVE TRAPPED YOU," BY MATTHEW BAILES, FROM *THE CONVERSATION*, FEBRUARY 26, 2013

The business model of many modern technology companies is to lure people into digital monopolies (or what are sometimes called "ecosystems") from whence ridiculous profits can be gouged.

You see, the internet and computing hardware, software and networking have become so fault-tolerant and scalable that it enables tremendous numbers of transactions per second to be completed without the need for expensive employees.

This can generate profit at hitherto unprecedented rates for what is little more than "file-sharing".

THE APPLE TV

At home we have an "Apple TV". It's an amazingly clever device, only costs about A$100 (+GST) and plugs into your TV set to allow you to watch movies and TV shows from the iTunes store in glorious HD via a wireless internet connection.

The beauty of the Apple TV is that it is very cheap and very tiny (see below).

Apple doesn't need to make any money from initially selling me the device, because most of the things I use it for make Apple more money.

Every time I rent a video or TV show Apple cashes in, and it's all done by computer, with little or no employees involved.

On Saturday I had the pleasure of watching *The Dark Knight Rises* on my Apple TV with my sons. Currently in Australia the movie costs A$24.99 but in the US only US$14.99. Now, you might wonder why copying a bunch of bits in a file to the Apple TV costs $10 more from Australia than the US, even though our dollar is worth more?

The answer is simple:

By purchasing an Apple TV I have trapped myself into a digital monopoly and they can get away with it.

I can't watch online movies legally in any other way without investing in someone else's device first. The barrier to switching movie providers is too high, so I stick with Apple.

I'm in their "ecosystem" and this is exactly where they want me.

This is really very different from how I used to watch movies, because anyone could sell me a video or DVD, which introduced competition – and the manufacturer was completely out of the picture after the initial purchase.

So what's the impact of this on the local economy?

WHITHER THE VIDEO STORE?

Once upon a time I used to go to the video shop and rent videos.

After an (often painful) family decision I would hand over my A$7 for a latest release, and sometimes more in late fees.

The owner of the video store paid some kid to man the store, paid rent to the shop's owner, and paid money to the Australian distributor. He or she then kept the profit after an initial outlay for the video/DVD.

My money was used for all sorts of purposes that helped stimulate the local economy and generate taxation.

Now I rent online and most of my money goes offshore and contributes to our foreign debt.

But this practice isn't limited to videos.

Every Tom, Dick and Harry is trying to trap us into digital monopolies or "ecosystems" that often suck money out of the country for little more that the transfer of information. As more of our disposable income goes towards the digital world, the more exposed we as a nation become.

Let's look at the iPhone/iPad or Android phones/tablets.

Once the initial hardware purchase has been made, every time we buy an "app" from the App Store or Google Play, 30% of the purchase price goes to Apple or Google respectively for doing little more than file-sharing after their initial investment in the hardware development.

Curiously, although Apple has made a bundle from this, it's true that software on the App Store is much cheaper than an equivalent game on a typical console.

That's because *anyone* can develop apps for the App Store but consoles generally restrict the number of people who can develop games to the select few willing to enter a relationship with the console creator.

Independent third parties are not allowed to write and distribute their own games for most consoles so that the consumer is forced to pay inflated prices for the software.

E-books are another example of growing digital ecosystems.

The wonderful Kindle tries very hard to get you to purchase from Amazon.

The cost of e-book distribution is almost nothing, and yet my only friend who writes bestsellers tells me that she only gets 25% of each e-book sale, with the "file sharer" getting the rest!

Is this fair?

BILLION DOLLAR PROFITS

Apple, being a public company, is forced to declare its profits, and has some amazing stats. In its latest proud declaration of record profits, Apple explains that the company posted record quarterly revenue of US$54.5 billion and a record quarterly net profit of US$13.1 billion.

This means on average almost 25% of each purchase is profit.

In fact Apple has made so much money that it has about US$140 billion cash in the bank.

THE FREE MARKET, REGULATIONS OR PEOPLE TO THE RESCUE?

Historically, when pricing becomes outrageous, other vendors enter "the space" and offer cheaper alternatives and competition drives down pricing (and profits).

But if anyone wants to take on Apple, they better be prepared to take on a company with more than US$100 billion to spend defending its profits.

Increasingly consumers are being sucked into purchasing devices that mandate the continued purchase from a monopoly or else the (expensive) device is useless.

With the coming of "the Cloud", where your content is stored elsewhere, if you ever abandon one vendor you might just torch your entire collection, making this problem even worse.

This is where governments should come in to protect consumers.

How many parents have been horrified at the cost of console games once the initial console purchase has been made?

Companies selling devices that lock you into buying software or content from a single vendor should be subject to different tax structures than open-source devices.

Alternatively the gouged users should rise up and found their own companies that develop open-source

WHAT ORDINARY PEOPLE SAY

hardware and platforms that anyone can provide content for, defeating the monopolies that increasingly abound in the digital world.

1. The author uses the Apple TV as an example of a monopolistic practice because Apple not only makes money off the device but also forces users to buy and rent the majority of their digital viewing content from Apple as well. Do you agree with this explanation?

2. The author later contends that while many parts of Apple are monopolistic, the company's app store allows all kinds of third-party developers to sell their apps and make money through the store. Do you think a company can have both good and bad business practices? If so, do you think Apple can be considered a monopoly if only parts of the company participate in monopolistic behavior?

"THE MONOPOLIES THAT NO ONE IS TALKING ABOUT," BY GABRIELLE DALEY, FROM *PUBLIC KNOWLEDGE*, SEPTEMBER 1, 2017

Recently there's been a lot of noise about monopolies and antitrust in the United States. The Federal Trade Commission approved Amazon's bid to buy Whole Foods in August, and Google was served with a record breaking fine by the

211

European Union's antitrust regulator in June. These stories have been fueling the buzz around competition policy discussions in the U.S. People are suddenly discussing the relevance of the Sherman Act, passed over 100 years ago. People are talking about whether there are "new monopolies" that these tech platforms could have on internet search, internet shopping, and more. But mostly, people are looking around and realizing that after waves of consolidation, the U.S. economy has a few big players at the top -- and fewer options when they need to buy something be it online or in their hometown.

Leaving aside the discussion for a minute on whether tech platforms like Google and Amazon actually might meet the definition of a monopoly under our nation's antitrust laws (a precise and economically rigorous definition usually left to the Department of Justice, the Federal Trade Commission, or the federal (and sometimes state) court system), we seem to have forgotten about an important part of the digital ecosystem and whether it has a monopoly problem. It's the one that's hiding in plain sight and the evidence is in your mailbox (or inbox) every month when you get your cable bill.

Why does is matter if cable internet service providers have market power? When companies monopolize they may hurt consumers because they no longer have the incentives to compete on price or service, with the unsurprising result that even while profits for companies increase consumer satisfaction plummets and prices continue to rise.

That cable internet service providers have terrible service ratings isn't anything new. The largest cable companies in the U.S seem to compete for the title of most disliked service provider, and hang out on the bottom of consumer satisfaction reports.

Customers don't seem surprised. And that's the problem. According to the Federal Communication Commission's latest Broadband Progress Report, most consumers only have once choice of broadband provider in their area, and so even with these poor ratings, consumers don't have another option when their current provider fails them.

Cable pricing is notoriously byzantine with an archaic list of charges and fees showing up on your bill every month that seem to bear little resemblance to the prices in their advertisements. Throw in the complications of bundling internet service with phone and TV, and it becomes unsurprising that cable providers have special sections on their websites for consumers trying to understand how to read their monthly bills and answer important questions like: Why did my bill go up?

But what happens when there actually is competition in this kind of market? We had a chance to observe some examples of what competition in broadband internet could look like with the growth of new internet offerings in the U.S. Starting in 2010, Google began offering super-fast broadband internet. Some cities like Chattanooga, Tennessee even began offering municipal broadband, including broadband at faster than ever speeds.

In 2016, the Fiber to the Home Council asked Analysis Group to conduct a study to see what was happening in the markets where cable internet companies actually were facing competition. It's a basic presumption of economics that where there is competition consumers will be better off. Would that actually hold true when we looked at the data? The report, released in November of 2016 and entitled Broadband Competition Helps to Drive Lower Prices and Faster Download Speeds for U.S. Residential Consumers, found that where cable internet service providers were competing with superfast internet offerings that prices were better for consumers. Not only did cable internet service providers offer higher speeds, but even the prices for lower speed tiers of service went down as well. According to the report where gigabit services are offered prices for standard plans offering speeds of 25Mbps to less than 1 Gbps decline by approximately $13-18, or 14-19 percent.

Cable internet service providers argue that they are already in a competitive market. They claim that DSL is a viable option that competes with their own services for customers. But that ignores the technical realities of these different technologies. In 2015 the FCC redefined broadband internet to take into account the needs of consumers as the way that we use the internet has changed. Now broadband internet service is defined as offerings with speeds of at least 25 mbps down and 3 up. These speeds allows consumers to stream video, listen to music and podcasts, make video calls, and connect smart devices around their homes. But this classification reflects that DSL is effectively no longer in the running, and consumers have limited choices for broadband.

It's important that we consider how technology platforms impact our lives and our patterns of consumption as we evaluate our nation's approach to competition. But we shouldn't allow those important issues to obscure this one: that most of us don't have enough choices when it comes to our cable broadband provider- and if we did, we could see real savings in our pocketbooks.

1. The author raises the question of whether cable companies can be considered monopolies because many have holds on their markets and aren't subject to competition. Do you think this lack of competition has been caused by monopolistic behavior by cable companies, or is it causing monopolistic behavior?

2. Antitrust laws are designed to help consumers from bad behavior by businesses. Do you think digital and technology companies can be held subject to the same laws as typical brick-and-mortar businesses? Why or why not?

CONCLUSION

While digital monopolies aren't quite the same as the railroad monopolies of the 1800s, which were the first to inspire antitrust laws in the United States, there's just as much danger in letting them run wild. Monopolies, as you've learned, whether they're in the digital landscape or the physical world, are harmful not only to other businesses, but to consumers.

As the internet becomes a bigger and bigger part of our everyday lives, digital monopolies are going to become more common, and more dangerous. But dealing with them won't be as easy as enacting a single antitrust law, as you've now learned. Not only do digital monopolies affect how people get online but what they do online, too.

If digital monopolies are allowed to flourish, things as simple as searching the internet for information will change. But is that a bad thing? That will be up to people like you to determine. You'll soon be tasked with deciding whether you're okay with Google and Facebook controlling online advertising and consumer information, whether you'll accept some people having only one internet service provider in their area, and whether you want to shop from only one website or have multiple options. And those are just the issues we're facing today. The more we rely on the internet, the more opportunity there is for other companies to develop online monopolies.

Figuring out how to deal with these changes will take a lot of consideration from not only you, but our government and our business leaders, and it won't be easy even if everyone agrees. But knowing about the problem is an important first step, and by finishing this book, you're now prepared to tackle this issue head-on.

BIBLIOGRAPHY

Bailes, Matthew. "Smash the Machine: Digital Monopolies Have Trapped You." *The Conversation*, February 26, 2013. https://theconversation .com/smash-the-machine-digital-monopolies-have-trapped-you-12496.

Daley, Gabrielle. "The Monopolies That No One Is Talking About." *Public Knowledge*, September 1, 2017. https://www.publicknowledge.org /news-blog/blogs/the-monopolies-that-no-one-is-talking-about.

Daniel, Michael. "Getting Serious About Information Sharing for Cybersecurity." The White House Archives, April 10, 2014. https:// obamawhitehouse.archives.gov/blog/2014/04/10/getting-seri-ous-about-information-sharing-cybersecurity.

Freedman, Des. "The Public Says: Break Big Media Monopolies and Help New Journalism Projects." *The Conversation*, April 1, 2015. https://the-conversation.com/the-public-says-break-big-media-monopolies-and -help-new-journalism-projects-39652.

Furman, Jason. "Beyond Antitrust: The Role of Competition Policy in Promoting Inclusive Growth." The White House Archives, September 16, 2016. https://obamawhitehouse.archives.gov/sites /default/files/page/files/20160916_searle_conference_competition_fur-man_cea.pdf.

Galperin, Hernán, Annette M. Kim and François Bar. "America's Broad-band Market Needs More Competition." *The Conversation*, March 5, 2017. https://theconversation.com/americas-broadband -market-needs-more-competition-71676.

Glance, David. "The EU's Obsession with Google Shows How Little It Understands the Digital Economy." *The Conversation*, November 30, 2014. https://theconversation.com/the-eus-obsession-with-google -shows-how-little-it-understands-the-digital-economy-34844.

Glaser, April and Corynne McSherry. "Neutrality Begins At Home: What U.S. Mayors Can Do Right Now to Support a Neutral Internet." *Electronic Frontier Foundation*, June 20, 2014. https://www.eff.org/deep-links/2014/06/neutrality-begins-home-what-us-mayors-can-do-right -now-support-neutral-internet.

Heinze, Aleksej and Evgenia Kanellopoulou. "EU Competition Watch-dogs Would Be Wise to Watch Out For Apple's Growth." *The Conversation*, November 28, 2014. https://theconversation.com /eu-competition-watchdogs-would-be-wise-to-watch-out-for-apples-growth-34714.

Hutchinson, Emma. "Principles of Microeconomics." The University of Victoria. BC Faculty Pressbooks Sites, 2016. https://pressbooks .bccampus.ca/uvicecon103.

Johnson, Jake. "As Tech Giants Threaten Democracy, Calls Grow for New Anti-Monopoly Movement." *Common Dreams*, September 1, 2017. https://www.commondreams.org/news/2017/09/01/tech-giants-threat-en-democracy-calls-grow-new-anti-monopoly-movement.

Johnson, Jake. "Google Fine Shows EU 'Way Ahead' of US on Reining in Massive Corporations." *Common Dreams*, June 27, 2017. https://www.commondreams.org/news/2017/06/27/google-fine-shows-eu-way-ahead-us-reining-massive-corporations.

Kollar-Kotelly, Colleen. "Final Judgments in *US v. Microsoft Corporation*." United States District Court for the District of Columbia. November 12, 2002. https://www.justice.gov/atr/case-document/final-judgment-133

Livingston, Debra Ann. *United States v. Apple, Inc.* Second US Circuit Court of Appeals, June 30, 2015. http://caselaw.findlaw.com/us-2nd-circuit/1706094.html

Lynn, Barry and Kevin Carty. "To Address Inequality, Let's Take on Monopolies." *Common Dreams*, September 22, 2017. https://www.commondreams.org/views/2017/09/22/address-inequality-lets-take-monopolies.

Moore, Martin. "After Years of Talk, a Regulator is Willing to Take on Google." *The Conversation*, April 30, 2015. https://theconversation.com/after-years-of-talk-a-regulator-is-willing-to-take-on-google-40861.

Newman, John. "Are US Antitrust Regulators Giving Silicon Valley's 'Free' Apps a Free Pass?" *The Conversation*, August 29, 2016. https://theconversation.com/are-us-antitrust-regulators-giving-silicon-valleys-free-apps-a-free-pass-63974.

Obama, Barack. "Executive Order — Steps to Increase Competition and Better Inform Consumers and Workers to Support Continued Growth of the American Economy." The White House Archives, April 15, 2016. https://obamawhitehouse.archives.gov/the-press-office/2016/04/15/executive-order-steps-increase-competition-and-better-inform-consumers.

Radu, Roxana and Jean-Marie Chenou. "Data Control and Digital Regulatory Space(s): Towards a New European Approach." *Internet Policy Review*. June 30, 2015. https://policyreview.info/articles/analysis/data-control-and-digital-regulatory-spaces-towards-new-european-approach.

Shiva, Vandana. "People's Economies vs Corporate Control: First Commodification, Then Financialization, Now Demonetization." *Common Dreams*, December 5, 2016. https://www.commondreams.org/views/2016/12/05/peoples-economies-vs-corporate-control-first-commodification-then-financialization.

Solomon, Norman. "Digital Grab: Corporate Power Has Seized the Internet." *Common Dreams,* March 28, 2013. https://www.commondreams.org/views/2013/03/28/digital-grab-corporate-power-has-seized-internet.

White, Andrew. "The Digital Economy is No Leveler, It's a Source of Inequality." *The Conversation*, January 26, 2015. https://theconversation.com/the-digital-economy-is-no-leveller-its-a-source-of-inequality-36714.

CHAPTER NOTES

CHAPTER 1: WHAT THE EXPERTS SAY

EXCERPT FROM "PRINCIPLES OF MICROECONOMICS," BY EMMA HUTCHINSON

Aboukhadijeh, Feross. "Chapter 20: Girding for War – The North and the South, 1861-1865." *StudyNotes, Inc*. Accessed July 7, 2013. http://www.apstudynotes.org/us-history/outlines/chapter-20-girding-for-war-the-north-and-the-south-1861-1865/.

Adam Ruins Everything. CollegeHumour. "Why Engagement Rings Are a Scam." February 13, 2014. http://www.collegehumor.com/video/6952792/why-engagement-rings-are-a-scam

British Parliament. "(28 August 1833). Slavery Abolition Act 1833; Section LXIV." Accessed July 2013. http://www.pdavis.nl/Legis_07.htm.

Dattel, E. (nd). "Cotton and the Civil War." *Mississippi Historical Society*. Accessed July 2013. http://mshistorynow.mdah.state.ms.us/articles/291/cotton-and-the-civil-war.

The Economist. "The Future of Forever: A Report from DeBeers New Diamond Mine." February 25, 2017. http://www.economist.com/news/international/21717369-production-worlds-most-valuable-gem-may-be-about-peak-report-de-beerss

Friedman, Uri. *The Atlantic*. "How an Ad Campaign Invented the Diamond Engagement Ring." February 13, 2015. https://www.theatlantic.com/international/archive/2015/02/how-an-ad-campaign-invented-the-diamond-engagement-ring/385376.

Massachusetts Historical Society. "The Coming of the American Revolution 1764-1776: The Boston Tea Party." Retrieved from http://www.masshist.org/revolution/teaparty.php.

Massachusetts Historical Society. "Whereas our Nation." *The Massachusetts Gazette*, p. 2. Accessed July 2013 http://www.masshist.org/revolution/image-viewer.php?old=1&item_id=457&img_step=1&nmask=1&mode=large.

Touryalai, Halah. *Forbes*. "Ray-Ban, Oakley, Chanel Or Prada

Sunglasses? They're All Made By This Obscure $9B Company." July 2, 2013. https://www.forbes.com/sites/halahtoury-alai/2013/07/02/ray-ban-oakley-chanel-or-prada-sunglasses-theyre-all-made-by-this-obscure-9b-company/#237511b364d6

CHAPTER 2: WHAT THE GOVERNMENT AND POLITICIANS SAY

"BEYOND ANTITRUST: THE ROLE OF COMPETITION POLICY IN PROMOTING INCLUSIVE GROWTH" BY JASON FURMAN

1. The Herfindahl - Hirschman Index (HHI) is a commonly used measure of market concentration that is created by summing up the squared shares of firms in a market. Higher values of the HHI indicate higher market concentration; it can be close to zero when a market is comprised of a large number of firms of small size and reaches a maximum of 10,000 when a market is controlled by a single firm. Antitrust agencies generally consider markets in which HHI is between 1,500 and 2,500 to be moderately concentrated, and consider markets in which the HHI is in excess of 2,500 to be highly concentrated (see https:// www.justice.gov/atr/herfindahl-hirschman-index for more detail).

REFERENCES

Abowd, John M. et al. 2012. "Persistent Inter-Industry Wage Differences: Rent Sharing and Opportunity Costs." IZA *Journal of Labor Economics* 1 (7).

Azmat, Ghazala, Alan Manning, and John Van Reenen. 2011. "Privatization and the Decline of Labour's Share: International Evidence from Network Industries." *Economica* 79 (315): 470- 492.

Barth, Erling, Alex Bryson, James C. Davis, and Richard Freeman. 2015. "Increases in Earnings Dispersion Across Establishments and Individuals in the U.S." NBER Working Paper No. 20447.

Bennett, Victor M., and Claudine M. Gartenberg. 2016. "Changes in Persistence of Performance Over Time." Working Paper.

Bentolila, Samuel, and Giles Saint-Paul. 2003. "Explaining Movements in the Labor Share." *B.E. Journal of Macroeconomics* 1 (3).

Blanchard, Olivier J., William D. Nordhaus, and Edmund S. Phelps. 1997. "The Medium Run." Brookings Papers on Economic Activity 1997 (2): 89-158.

Campbell, John Y., Carolin Pflueger, and Luis Viceira. 2014. "Monetary Policy Drivers of Bond and Equity Risks." NBER Working Paper No. 20070.

Chetty, Raj, et al. 2014. "Where is the Land of Opportunity? The Geography of Intergenerational Mobility in the United States." National Bureau of Economic Research Working Paper 19843.

Chetty, Raj, et al. 2015. "The Effects of Exposure to Better Neighborhoods on Children: New Evidence from the Moving to Opportunity Experiment." National Bureau of Economic Research Working Paper 21156.

Corbae, Dean and Pablo D'Erasmo. 2013. "A Quantitative Model of Banking Industry Dynamics."

Council of Economic Advisers (CEA). 2015. "Worker Voice in a Time of Rising Inequality." Issue brief.

Davis, Steven J., and John Haltiwanger. 2014. "Labor Market Fluidity and Economic Performance." NBER Working Paper No. 20479.

Decker, Ryan, John Waltiwanger, Ron S. Jarmin, and Javier Miranda. 2014. "The Secular Decline in Business Dynamism in the U.S." Working Paper Presented at Heritage Foundation Center for Data Analysis.

Department of the Treasury Office of Economic Policy, Council of Economic Advisers, and Department of Labor. 2015. "Occupational Licensing: A Framework for Policymakers." Report.

The Economist. 2016. "Too Much of a Good Thing."

Elsby, Michael W.L., Bart Hobijn, and Aysegul Sahin. 2013. "On the Importance of the Participation Margin for Market Fluctuations."

Federal Reserve Bank of San Francisco Working Paper No. 2013-05. Federal Communications Commission. 2015. "Eighteenth Annual Report and Analysis of Competitive Market Conditions With Respect to Mobile Wireless, Including Commercial Mobile Services." Report.

Furman, Jason. 2015. "Barriers to Shared Growth: The Case of Land Use Regulation and Economic Rents." Remarks at Urban Institute.

Furman, Jason, and Peter Orszag. 2015. "A Firm-Level Perspective on the Role of Rents in the Rise in Inequality." Paper presented at Columbia University's "A Just Society" Centennial Event in Honor of Joseph Stiglitz, New York, NY.

Gaynor, Martin, Kate Ho, and Robert J. Town. 2015. "The Industrial Organization of HealthCare Markets." *Journal of Economic Literature* 53 (2): 235-84.

Gibbons, Robert and Lawrence Katz. 1992. "Does Unmeasured Ability Explain Inter-Industry Wage Differentials?" *Review of Economic Studies* 59: 515-535.

Glaeser, Edward L., and Joseph Gyourko. 2003. "The Impact of Building Restrictions on Housing Affordability." *Economic Policy Review* 9 (2): 21-39.

Gyourko, Joseph, and Raven Molloy. 2015. "Regulation and Housing Supply." in Duranton, Gilles, J. Vernon Henderson, and William C. Strange eds., *Handbook of Regional and Urban Economics*. Volume 5B. Handbook of Regional and Urban Economics. Amsterdam; San Diego and Oxford: Elsevier Science.

Harrison, Ann. 2005. "Has Globalization Eroded Labor's Share? Some Cross-Country Evidence." Munich Personal RePEc Archive.

Hyatt, Henry R., and James R. Spletzer. 2013. "The Recent Decline in Employment Dynamics." U.S. Census Bureau Center for Economic Studies Discussion Paper No. 13-03.

Jarsulic, Marc, Ethan Gurwitz, Kate Bahn, and Andy Green. 2016. "Reviving Antitrust: Why Our Economy Needs Progressive Competition Policy." Center for American Progress Report.

Jaumotte, Florence, and Irina Tytell. 2007. "How Has the Globalization of Labor Affected the Labor Income Share in Advanced Countries?" IMF Working Paper No. 07-298.

Kaldor, Nicholas. 1957. "A Model of Economic Growth." *The Economic Journal* 67 (268): 591- 624.

Kaplan, Greg, and Sam Schulhofer-Wohl. 2015. "Understanding the Long-Run Decline in Interstate Migration." Federal Reserve Bank of Minneapolis Working Paper No. 697.

Karabarbounis, Loukas and Brent Neiman. 2013. "The Global Decline of the Labor Share." NBER Working Paper No. 19136.

Kleiner, Morris, and Alan Krueger. 2013. "Analyzing the Extent and Influence of Occupational Licensing on the Labor Market." *Journal of Labor Economics* 31 (2): S173-202.

Kozlowski, Julian, Laura Veldkamp, and Venky Venkateswaran. 2015. "The Tail That Wags the Economy: Belief-Driven Business Cycles and Persistent Stagnation." NBER Working Paper No. 21719.

Krueger, Alan B. and Lawrence H. Summers. 1988. "Efficiency Wages and the Inter-Industry Wage Structure." *Econometrica* 56 (2): 259-293.

Manning, Alan. 2003. *Monopsony in Motion: Imperfect Competition in Labor Markets.* Princeton NJ: Princeton UP.

Molloy, Raven S., Christopher L. Smith, Riccardo Trezzi, and Abigail Wozniak. 2016. "Understanding Declining Fluidity in the U.S. Labor Market." Brookings Papers on Economic Activity, BPEA Conference Draft, March 10-11. Brookings Institute.

Molloy, Raven S., Christopher L. Smith, and Abigail K. Wozniak. 2014. "Declining Migration within the US: The Role of the Labor Market."

National Bureau of Economic Research Working Paper 20065. U.S. Department of the Treasury, Office of Economic Policy. 2016.

"Non-compete Contracts: Economic Effects and Policy Implications." Report.

Prater, Marvin E., Ken Casavant, Eric Jessup, Bruce Blaton, Pierre Bahizi, Daniel Nibarger, and Isaac Weingram. 2012. "Rail Competition Changes Since the Staggers Act." *Journal of the Transportation Research Forum* 49 (3): 111-132.

Shields, Dennis A. 2010. "Consolidation and Concentration in the U.S. Dairy Industry." Congressional Research Service. Report for Congress.

Smith, Adam. 1776. *An Inquiry into the Nature and Causes of the Wealth of Nations.*

Starr, Evan, JJ Prescott, and Norman Bishara (2016): "Noncompetes in the U.S. Labor Force." Working Paper.

CHAPTER 3: WHAT THE COURTS SAY

"UNITED STATES V. APPLE, INC." BY CIRCUIT JUDGE DEBRA ANN LIVINGSTON

1. The factual background presented here is drawn from the district court's factual findings or from undisputed material in the record before the district court. Because this Court reviews the district court's factual findings for "clear error," we must assess whether "its view of the evidence is plausible in light of the entire record." *Cosme v. Henderson*, 287 F.3d 152, 158 (2d Cir. 2002). In light of this obligation, the dissent is wrong to suggest that citations to the record are inappropriate or misleading. When a fact comes from the district court's opinion, we cite that opinion; when one comes from the record, we cite the joint appendix ("J.A.").

2. Citing one example, the district court referenced a fall 2009 email in which Hachette's Young informed his colleague Nourry of Simon & Schuster's windowing plans, advising "[c]ompletely confidentially, Carolyn [Reidy] has told me that they [Simon & Schuster] are delaying the new Stephen King, with his full support, but will not be announcing this until the day after Labor

Day." *Apple*, 952 F. Supp. 2d at 652 (first and second alterations in original) (internal quotation marks omitted). The district court went on to observe that Young, "[u]nderstanding the impropriety of this exchange of confidential information with a competitor, . . . advised Nourry that 'it would be prudent for you to double delete this from your email files when you return to your office.'" *Id.*

3. Notably, the possibility of an agency arrangement was first mentioned by Hachette and HarperCollins as a way "to fix Amazon pricing." J.A. 346

4. Cue testified at trial that his reference to "solv[ing] the Amazon issue" denoted the proposal to price ebooks in the iBookstore above $9.99, and was not a reference to raising prices across the industry or wresting control over pricing from Amazon. In this and other respects, the district court found Cue's testimony to be "not credible" — a determination that, on this record, is in no manner erroneous, much less clearly so. *Id.* at 661 n.19. As the district court put it, "Apple's pitch to the Publishers was — from beginning to end — a vision for a new industry-wide price schedule." *Id.*

5. As one HarperCollins executive put it, the "upshot" of moving to the agency model and adopting price caps was that "Apple would control price and that price would be standard across the industry." *Apple*, 952 F. Supp. 2d at 670 (internal quotation marks omitted).

6. Although Cue denied discussing the MFN that night, the district court found this testimony not credible in light of Cue's deposition testimony and his contemporaneous email to Jobs that Sargent had "legal concerns over the price- matching." Apple, 952 F. Supp. 2d at 672 n.38 (internal quotation marks omitted). This determination was not clearly erroneous.

7. Indeed, on the morning of January 21, Apple's initial deadline for the publishers to commit to agency, Simon & Schuster's Reidy emailed Cue to get "an update on your progress in herding us cats." J.A. 543.

8. On January 29, Simon & Schuster's general counsel wrote to Reidy that she "[could not] believe that Jobs made [this] statement," which she considered "[i]ncredibly stupid." J.A. 638.

9. As the district court found, "[s]even months was no random period — it was the number of months for which titles were designated New Release titles under the Apple Agreement and restrained by the Apple price caps and MFN." *Apple*, 952 F. Supp. 2d at 679.

10. At trial, Cue claimed he had no advance knowledge of Sargent's plan to go to Seattle, but the district court found this testimony to be incredible. Sargent had emailed Cue about his trip days before the meeting took place. Moreover, on January 28, the day of the meeting, Jobs told his biographer that the Publisher Defendants "went to Amazon and said, 'You're going to sign an agency contract or we're not going to give you the books.'" *Apple*, 952 F. Supp. 2d at 678 n.47. The district court's assessment of Cue's credibility was not clearly erroneous.

11. As the district court noted, Macmillan had executed its Contract with Apple a week earlier, so that "the only final agency terms still under discussion were with Amazon." *Apple*, 952 F. Supp. 2d at 681 n.52.

12. Eventually, the Publisher Defendants negotiated agency agreements with Barnes & Noble, and later Google. Random House also adopted the agency model, and joined the iBookstore, in early 2011.

13. The five Publisher Defendants accounted for 48.8% of all retail trade ebook sales in the United States during the first quarter of 2010.

14. A weighted average price controls for the fact that different ebooks sell in different quantities by dividing the total price that consumers paid for ebooks by the total number of ebooks sold.

GLOSSARY

antitrust laws—Laws that prevent companies from growing too big and powerful, and that help consumers by promoting competition among businesses.

brick-and-mortar—A business that exists in the physical as opposed to digital world; a physical bookstore as opposed to Amazon's Kindle bookstore, for example.

broadband—A kind of internet connection that uses high-speed connections, such as fiber optics or radio transmissions.

competition—When two or more businesses must fight to gain customers by outdoing one another, either by providing better service or lower prices, among other things.

cybersecurity—Protection for your digital or online life.

ebook—A book that is created as a digital file and can be read on a device like a tablet or a special e-book device known as an e-reader.

e-commerce—A business that takes place entirely online and that doesn't involve any real-world interactions; even payment happens digitally and does not involve actual, physical money.

European Union—A collection of European countries that act together politically and economically to promote better relations across Europe.

executive order—An order from the president of the United States that creates a law without having to first go through Congress.

internet service provider—A company that helps customers connect to the internet by selling them a connection.

monopolistic—Any behavior that is enacted with the hope or result of creating a monopoly.

monopoly—A situation is which a company gets most or all of consumers' business in a particular field; for example, Google is believed to have a monopoly on online search traffic.

net neutrality—The belief that all online media should be treated equally when being transmitted to users; no one type of media, such a certain websites or media files, should be treated differently than others by internet service providers.

software—A digital program that can be used on a computer, tablet, or phone but that does not require a physical change to the device to be used.

FOR MORE INFORMATION

FURTHER READING

Bagdikian, Ben H. *The New Media Monopoly*. New York, NY: Beacon Press, 2004.

Manning, Alan. *Monopsony in Motion: Imperfect Competition in Labor Markets*. Princeton, NJ: Princeton University Press, 2003.

McChesney, Robert W. *Digital Disconnect: How Capitalism Is Turning the Internet Against Democracy*. New York, NY: The New Press, 2014.

Moazed, Alex and Nicholas L. Johnson. *Modern Monopolies: What It Takes to Dominate the 21st Century Economy*. New York, NY: St. Martin's Press, 2016.

Rushkoff, Douglas. *Throwing Rocks at the Google Bus: How Growth Became the Enemy of Prosperity*. New York, NY: Portfolio, 2016.

WEBSITES

American Antitrust Institute
http://www.antitrustinstitute.org
The American Antitrust Institute is an independent, nonprofit organization dedicated to promoting competition that protects consumers, businesses, and society. Their website features reports of market competition and research, among other resources.

Electronic Freedom Foundation
https://www.eff.org
The Electronic Freedom Foundation is a leading nonprofit working to protect digital privacy and freedom, including preventing digital monopolies. Founded in 1990, the EFF uses litigation, policy analysis, and grassroots activism to ensure that human rights are protected as the digital space grows.

Public Knowledge
https://www.publicknowledge.org
Public Knowledge is a nonprofit organization that promotes freedom of expression and the free use of digital spaces. As such, their website features updates and articles about monopolies and antitrust regulations.

INDEX

ABOUT THE EDITOR

Jennifer Peters is a writer and editor whose work has focused on everything from relationships to books to military and defense issues. During her more than ten years working in the media, her work has appeared in a number of magazines and online news and culture sites, with her most recent bylines appearing on *VICE News* and *Task & Purpose*. She lives in Washington, DC, and she never leaves home without a good book.